Summer Fun

Summer Fun

*The Parents' Complete Guide
to Day Camps, Overnight Camps,
Specialty Camps, and Teen Tours*

Marian Edelman Borden

Facts On File, Inc.

Summer Fun: The Parents' Complete Guide to Day Camps, Overnight Camps, Specialty Camps, and Teen Tours

Copyright © 1999 by Marion Edelman Borden

Checkmark Books
An imprint of Facts On File, Inc.
11 Penn Plaza
New York NY 10001

Library of Congress Cataloging-in-Publication Data

Borden, Marion Edelman.
   Summer Fun : the parents' complete guide to day camps, overnight
camps, specialty camps, teen tours / by Marion Edelman Borden.
      p.   cm.
   Includes bibliographical references (p.   ) and index.
   ISBN 0-8160-3804-X (hc.).   ISBN 0-8160-3805-8 (pbk.)
   1. Camps—United States—Guidebooks.   I. Title.
GV193.B67   1999   98—38252
796.54'2'02573—dc21

Checkmark Books are available at special discounts when purchased in bulk quantities for businesses, associations, institutions, or sales promotions. Please call our Special Sales Department in New York at (212) 967-8800 or (800) 322-8755.

You can find Facts On File on the World Wide Web at http://www.factsonfile.com

Text design by Sandra Watanabe
Cover design by Maria Ilardi

Printed in the United States of America

MP FOF 10 9 8 7 6 5 4 3 2 1
(pbk)   10 9 8 7 6 5 4 3 2 1

This book is printed on acid-free paper.

For my sister Rachel,
who was with me when I first went to camp...
and with love and gratitude
for her support in all the years since.

Contents

1 Chapter 1

Day Camp: Summer Fun Begins

A day camp program is a perfect introduction to the camp experience for a young child, but it also may be just the right place for the older youngster who is not ready or uninterested in sleepaway camp. Here is a clear guide that lists the advantages and disadvantages of the wide range of day camp programs available. There is a full discussion of how to evaluate the camps and the essentials of a good day camp program. More expensive is not necessarily better—here's how to judge whether you're getting your money's worth.

29 Chapter 2

Sleepaway Camps: Fun Plus

For the older camper, ready for a new challenge, sleepaway camp may be the perfect answer. How do you know if your child is ready for this new experience? In this chapter you'll find clear readiness guidelines. Suppose your child is eager to go to sleepaway camp, but he's a bed wetter. Here's advice from experts who know. You'll also find a full discussion of the advantages and disadvantages of single sex and coed camps, general interest and specialty camps. Suggestions about session length, distance from home, budget considerations, and much more are included—all the basics you need to consider before beginning the search for the right sleep-away camp.

47 Chapter 3
Finding the Right Sleepaway Camp: The Search Can Be Fun

Here's a step-by-step guide that takes you from the yellow pages (look under camps) to contract. It presents national guidelines for safety and what to look for when you visit a camp. It's not just a question of what you see: What you don't see may be even more important! Included are checklists, expert advice, and parent tips for evaluating sleepaway camps. This information lets you become a camp expert.

69 Chapter 4
Ready, Set, Go: The Fun Begins

You've chosen the camp—now what? This chapter will give you all the information you need to organize, shop, pack, and ship your child's belongings to camp—what your camper really needs—and what's optional. Also, what you can do to ensure that most, if not all, of the belongings return home at the end of the summer. But getting ready for camp is more than buying the right clothes. Here's a full discussion of how to psychologically prepare your camper (and you) for sleepaway camp.

91 Chapter 5
Keeping in Touch: Sharing the Fun

The letters you send, the care packages you prepare, the visit on parents' weekend—all are ways of staying in touch with your camper. Here's what to say—and when. Homesickness? It's almost universal. Here's what works to help your camper over-come the blues. Plus how to handle birthdays and problems from a distance.

Specialty Camps: A Unique Kind of Fun

Your child may want or need a specialty camp. There are summer programs designed for almost any interest your child may have. There are camps for budding entrepreneurs, sports stars (and wanna-bes), space camps, theater camps, and nature camps. Name an interest or hobby, and undoubtedly there is a camp for it. And for the child with a chronic or life-threatening illness or learning disability, there are camps to help adjust to the disease, build a peer support network, and develop self-confidence and coping skills. In this chapter, parents will find the information they need to judge the safety and strength of these specialized camps. There are many more of these camps available than you might imagine. Here's how to evaluate if they're right for your child.

Teen Tours and More: The Fun Continues in Adolescence

Teenagers present a special challenge for finding summer fun that is appropriate, safe, and rewarding. This chapter reviews the many teen options for summer (including a paying job!). Here's how to evaluate teen tours, biking and camping trips, academic summer programs, volunteer opportunities, and more. Additionally, there are tips for communicating with your teenager so that you can share the summer fun.

Day Camp Evaluation Sheet

Overnight Camp Evaluation Sheet

Preface

Summer camp is more than a place—it's an experience that can be magical. More than 8 million kids discover this each year, and the numbers are growing. Why? First, and foremost, because camp is fun. It's kids playing, growing, and learning under the guidance of trained, caring camp directors and counselors.

Camp is a place to build lifetime memories because it offers everything a child must have to move successfully into adulthood. Camp encourages kids to try new activities and expand their horizons in a safe environment built specifically for them. At camp, kids learn how to get along with others and take responsibility for themselves. Camp is a time when children grow emotionally, socially, intellectually, physically, and often spiritually—all within a safe, secure, supportive atmosphere. Camp provides opportunities for kids to develop a sense of teamwork and independence, to develop and refine social skills, and to build self-confidence and self-esteem through accomplishment. And best of all—kids love it because it's fun!

Whether you are looking for a half-day program for your five-year-old, a traditional residential camp for your ten-year-old, a teen travel tour, or a special interest program, there is a camp for every child and for every budget. Good camps come in all shapes and sizes. But strong programs, whether they are in the cool woods, by a lake, or in a classroom in the city, whether they have a 100 kids or 700, share a common commitment to the development and enrichment of young people. Camp directors and staff believe in—and enjoy—kids. Their programs reflect that.

There are many excellent camps, but you need to match the needs of your child and family to the right program. *Summer Fun* can help. As you read this guide, you'll find the tools you'll need to choose the right camp for your child. You'll also learn how to prepare your camper, and yourself, for an exciting summer. There are practical, camper/parent-tested tips on packing, care packages, homesickness control, and more. *Summer Fun* will guide new campers and their families through this exciting experience.

Making the right choice is often a matter of asking the right questions. *Summer Fun* will take you on a journey that will lead to a safe, stimulating, and enjoyable experience.

—BOB SCHULTZ
Director of Development and Public Relations,
American Camping Association

Introduction

Summer camps are an American institution dating back to the early 1900s. Getting youngsters out of the city to enjoy the clean, cool air of the country during the sweltering summer months was the modest beginning of this national enterprise. Camps and campsites have changed dramatically in the intervening years. At today's summer camp, you are as likely to find a computer as a campfire; there may be a Rollerblade rink adjacent to the nature trail; a climbing wall and zip line may be surrounded by towering 200-year-old pines. In fact, while many wonderful summer camps are still located in the country, you can also find enriching summer camp programs in the middle of a city.

But appearances aside, the *essence* of the summer camp experience hasn't changed in the last 100 years. It's still about kids filling the long, lazy, hazy days of summer with fun and excitement, as they face new experiences and confront new challenges. Spending the summer at a good camp helps build a child's independence, self-confidence, and self-esteem. In a fun, relaxed atmosphere, the camper learns new skills and meets new friends, creating memories to last a lifetime.

According to a new study by the American Camping Association (ACA), an independent organization that accredits summer camps based on nationally accepted standards for health, safety, and program quality, enrollment in camp is up. Families are rediscovering that summer camp teaches, not only traditional skills like tennis, swimming, arts and crafts, but also *life skills*—lessons that last a lifetime.

Today, there are about 8,500 camps in the United States, 60 percent of which are sleepaway camps. Approximately 8 million children will attend camp each summer. Nonprofit organizations sponsor 70 percent of the camps; privately owned camps account for about 25 percent; and corporations, such as Nike's tennis camps, make up the remainder.

Experts estimate that the privately owned, for profit camps are an $11-billion industry. One study calculated that the average gross revenue per camp at over $1.1 million per season, but pointed out that the overhead and expenses of running a camp are enormous. Insurance, staff, marketing, food, site and facilities maintenance can easily push the costs up to $750,000 to $1 million a year, excluding mortgage payments. Some private camps make more, others less, depending on costs and revenues.

The business of running a camp is year-round, with marketing, recruitment, and site improvements dominating the off-season. But during the two months of summer, sleepaway camp owners work 24 hours, seven days a week. For day camp owners, during season, the hours aren't much shorter.

From the modest beginning of wanting to expose city children to healthy, outdoor living, summer camps have diversified and expanded so that today there is a camp that meets the needs of almost every child. While traditional (general interest) camps continue to dominate the market, you can also find specialty camps of all shapes and sizes. A partial listing of specialty camps (see chapter 6 for a more complete discussion) would include those that focus on individual sports (such as basketball, baseball, hockey, tennis, soccer, field hockey, etc.); academics; computers; dance; weight loss; chess; entrepreneurship; space; special needs; chronic illnesses; world peace; nature; environment. The list is endless.

There's also a camp to meet almost every budget. Recreation programs sponsored by local government can cost under $200 for the season. Day camps can range from $100 to $800 per week. Sleepaway camp fees run between $3,500 to $7,000 for an eight-week season, with some camps offering two-, four-, and six-week sessions proportionately priced. Specialty camps can cost from $350 to $800 per week depending on the program.

Choosing the right summer camp for each of my four children was the inspiration for this book. My kids have had some wonderful summer camp experiences, where they made new friends, learned new skills, tried new activities (some of which they loved, and some not), and ended the summer vacation refreshed and renewed, self-confidence abrimming.

And then there was the summer that my oldest son primarily learned how to play poker, traded baseball cards, and acquired a salty language. It was *not* what I would have defined as an enriching experience—although he might disagree!

Choosing the right summer program for your child does take time—and it's a decision that you may have to rethink each year. The right camp for your preschooler, even if it continues through adolescence, may not be the right place for a teenager—or more precisely *your* teenager. In *Summer Fun* you'll find a practical, *parent-tested* guide to choosing the right summer program for kids from 3 to 17. For kids with special needs and/or special interests, there's comprehensive information on how to evaluate these kinds of programs.

This book wouldn't have been possible without the help and cooperation of many families, campers, camp directors, counselors, and camp advisers who shared their stories and wisdom so that parents can make informed choices.

Special thanks to Bob Schultz of the American Camping Association who provided information and insight into the nitty-gritty and *the spirit* of summer camps. I especially appreciate the help of Andrew Townsend, director of Kennolyn Camps in Soquel, California; Maddy Feinberg, director of camps at the Mid-Westchester Y in Scarsdale, New York; and Rachel Glaser, business manager of Camp Moshava in Bel Air, Maryland; who shared with me—and with hundreds of children each summer—their enthusiasm and love for camping. Thanks too to Janice Millman of the Student Camp and Trip Advisors in Fairfield, Connecticut, who understands kids—and teens—and does a great job matching them to the right summer camp program. And much appreciation to Jeff Solomon of the National Camp Association who is always there to help families find the perfect program for their child, and to John Richard Tesone, director of Breezemont Day Camp in Armonk, New York, who has spent over 30 years in the business and shared his knowledge and enthusiasm for camping so graciously. Special thanks too must go to Jacquie Dickinson, executive director of Camp Ho Mita Koda, Cleveland, Ohio, for her assistance with the section on special needs camps.

Dr. Richard Silberg, a pediatrician, father of three campers, and enthusiastic camp doctor himself, was enormously helpful with health and safety questions. Thanks, too, to Winnie, Laura, and Adam Borden; Wendy, Herb, and Larry Brooks; Michael and Betsey Cherkasky; Laurie Edelman; Gail Friedman; Mary and Larry Goldman; Susan Jo Gordon;

Amy Kriss; Paula Krenkel; Andrew Levi; Sylvia and Rachel Posner; Barbara Rosenblum; Kate Kelly Schweitzer; Andrea Selonick; Toby and Bob Sklarew; Ronni and Scott Wadler; Marlo Wiggans; and Ellen Zuckert for their good humor and valuable insight into summer camps.

Special thanks to the team at Facts On File: Laurie Likoff, my editor, for her support and enthusiasm for this project, and Lisa Milberg and Kate Moore, for all their creative efforts.

Finally, as always, it's my husband John who always makes these books possible. Without his editorial advice, emotional support, and handling of the "details" at crunch time, the research and writing of this guide could not have been done. For Charlie, Sam, Dan, and Maggie, thanks for serving as the inspiration for these books, but most of all, for being the best kids a mom could ever have. And for Rachel, my big sister, thanks for the summer camp experiences—and for all your support in the years since.

To the parents searching for the right summer camp program for their child—good luck. The process of choosing the camp can be a wonderful experience to share with your child. And the joy and excitement on your child's face from experiencing the right summer program, makes all the effort worthwhile.

Summer Fun

Chapter 1

DAY CAMP:
SUMMER FUN BEGINS

We had just moved to a new community and my six-year-old looked like a lost soul. Although we had all the expenses of a new house, I just knew if he spent the long summer vacation with me at home, we both would be miserable. Luckily there was a nearby day camp. I checked it out with neighbors and signed my son up. What a relief. The first day he came home and told me about his new best friend. When he learned how to swim that summer as well, I felt like we had hit the jackpot.

Day camp is a perfect introduction for a young child to the camp experience, but it also may be just the right place for the older youngster who is not ready for or uninterested in sleepaway camp. In a good day camp program, young children have fun, even learn, all within the context of play. The older day camper experiences and explores many of the same activities campers enjoy in a sleepaway program, but with the reassurance and comfort of returning to home base at night.

There are approximately 3,000 day camps in the United States, although the numbers probably do not accurately reflect the local summer recreation programs or specialty clinics available in many communities. Finding the right program for your child takes time and effort, but

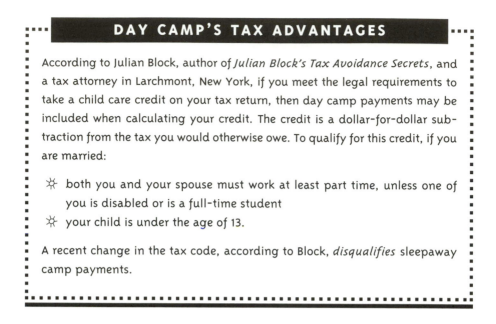

DAY CAMP'S TAX ADVANTAGES

According to Julian Block, author of *Julian Block's Tax Avoidance Secrets*, and a tax attorney in Larchmont, New York, if you meet the legal requirements to take a child care credit on your tax return, then day camp payments may be included when calculating your credit. The credit is a dollar-for-dollar sub-traction from the tax you would otherwise owe. To qualify for this credit, if you are married:

☀ both you and your spouse must work at least part time, unless one of you is disabled or is a full-time student
☀ your child is under the age of 13.

A recent change in the tax code, according to Block, *disqualifies* sleepaway camp payments.

is worth it when your youngster returns home at night with a smile on his face and tales of fun to relate.

FOR THE YOUNG CAMPER

What's the right age to enroll your child in camp? It depends on the program, your child, your budget, and your family's needs. Choosing the right summer camp for a young child under the age of five is similar to choosing a good preschool program. You want an environment where the counselors understand how young children learn and interact. You want a place that appreciates the developmental needs of young children and where the expectations of behavior are appropriate for the age group.

The Day Camp Program for Young Children

Like a good preschool, a day camp for preschoolers focuses on *play*. Children this age are just *learning* how to function independently; they are developing social skills; camp activities should build a child's self-esteem. Counselors need to understand issues of separation anxiety. For the young camper, this may be the first group experience she has and much like the preschool program, separation has to be done sensitively.

One mother enrolled her three-year-old in her town's morning day camp program. The youngster cried every morning, for three days in a row, and the mother could tell that the counselors, all high school students, were losing patience. She called the family pediatrician who recommended withdrawing the child from the program. "Those high school kids aren't trained to handle separation problems of preschoolers," the doctor pointed out.

That's not to say that local recreation programs can't be good. Some put the time and effort into recruiting qualified staffers and training them. In looking for a day camp program for a child under six, how the staff deals with separation issues is a good indication of their knowledge of young children. Many good day camp programs hire preschool teachers as supervisors/head counselors for this age group. *You also know your child. If she has attended preschool or day care prior to beginning camp, she may adapt more easily and separation issues may not arise.*

Scaled to Size

In a day camp program for young children, competition is minimal. Games focus on fun rather than winners. Counselors are comforting and nurturing. The toys, books, games, and equipment available in a day camp program for young children should be age and size appropriate.

Ideally, a day camp that accepts a wide age range of children (e.g., 3 to 12) will separate the younger from the older children. As a veteran camp professional with 33 years of experience points out, "We run a camp within a camp for our preschoolers. Young children are inhibited around older kids. Our preschoolers swim in their own two-and-a-half-foot pool, play on their own playground with equipment that is appropriate for younger children, eat lunch at a separate time. You have to understand how young children think. For example, little kids are afraid they're going to get trampled by the big kids if they're on the basketball court at the same time."

The camp day should include many of the components of a good preschool program.

☀ There is a strong emphasis on *free play* where the child chooses which activity or area she wants.
☀ Art projects should be tailored to meet the small motor development of young children. The emphasis should be on self-expression rather than fancy projects.

☼ Playground time is vital.

☼ Swimming lessons, if offered, must be taught by instructors who are experienced working with preschoolers. These water safety instructors must understand the physical and intellectual development of young children and tailor the lessons to this age group. There should be an emphasis on becoming comfortable in the water rather than a focus on specific strokes or breathing. And most of all instructors must be sensitive to the fears of young children and react accordingly. As one camp director explains, "Our goal is for the little kids to be happy and unafraid in the water. There's time for swim lessons later."

Full Day or Half-Day?

You will want to consider the age and energy level of your child when choosing between a half- or full-day program. Include travel time in your decision about the length of the camp day. Especially if your child is traveling by camp bus, it can lengthen the day by a half hour or more.

A full-day program generally begins at 9 A.M. and ends at 4 P.M. But with bus time, it can begin as early as 7:30 A.M. (for example, for kids who are traveling from Manhattan to a suburban day camp), and end after 5 P.M. That's a long day for a preschooler. You may decide you prefer a half-day program, which generally ends around noon or 1 P.M.

You may want to increase the length of the program as your child gets older, perhaps starting off with a half-day schedule for young preschoolers, threes and fours, and switching to a full-day program for kindergartners and older.

Even if you have a high-energy-level child, one who seems to be on the run almost constantly or who is looking for another play date before the first one has left, don't underestimate how demanding day camp can be. Besides the physical requirements of an exciting, high quality program that has a strong outdoor component, there is also the psychological stress. A young child has to separate from her parents/caregiver, maintain her composure, learn to share adult attention and materials, focus on new tasks and activities, interact with peers, and cope with self-competency issues like dressing and toileting. This is a lot for a young child to sustain over a long period of time. It's the reason why many preschoolers, those who have long ago given up their daily naps, may come home from day camp and either sleep or need a quiet rest period in the afternoon. They need downtime.

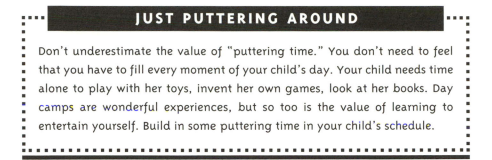

JUST PUTTERING AROUND

Don't underestimate the value of "puttering time." You don't need to feel that you have to fill every moment of your child's day. Your child needs time alone to play with her toys, invent her own games, look at her books. Day camps are wonderful experiences, but so too is the value of learning to entertain yourself. Build in some puttering time in your child's schedule.

If you select a full-day program for your young child, ask the camp if they schedule a rest period or at least a quiet time during the day. Many build in a *quiet* time after lunch when the children may rest on mats (many actually fall asleep) or at least play or look at books quietly.

For families who need the day camp to provide them with the child care they need, finding the right length program may be difficult. You need to assess your own child's stamina and make alternative plans if you think a full-day program is too much.

FOR THE OLDER CHILD

When looking for a day camp for an older child you are generally less concerned about separation issues. That's not to say that a seven-year-old won't be nervous about starting a new program with strange kids. She may well be, and you need a trained staff that works to make every child comfortable and feeling like part of the group. But by age six or seven, most children are in school all day and are more comfortable separating from home base. They may not be ready for sleepaway camp, but a full-day program is reasonable, and the range of activities and experiences can be more challenging.

For the older child, you still need to ask questions about the daily program and activities, as well as check references.

CHOOSING A DAY CAMP

Choosing the right day camp for your child requires you to visit, observe, and evaluate what you see *and what you don't see.* Some of what you observe is quantifiable: the qualifications of the staff; whether or not the camp is accredited and licensed by the appropriate local and state boards; the age and condition of the equipment and facilities; the availability of a gym or some large space for indoor days.

And some of the evaluation will be on a *gut level*, your own best instincts about the people you meet and how your child will fit in.

How to Start?

Here are some ways to find camps in your area.

- ☀ Of course, *word of mouth* is generally the best resource. Other families in your community may recommend or criticize a local day camp. Consider the source and listen carefully to the comments. Any problems reported may not be an issue for you or may reflect different child-rearing practices or expectations.
- ☀ Check your *church or synagogue*. Many religious institutions either sponsor a day camp or rent space to a program.
- ☀ The local *YMCA* or *YMHA* may also house day camp programs.
- ☀ Your *pediatrician* is another good resource for local programs.
- ☀ Call your *local recreation commission* to find out about any public day camp or recreation programs. Many are housed in the local elementary schools or parks.
- ☀ Go *on-line* and check with parenting forums. Many parents post queries about their specific geographic area on bulletin boards and get responses from other local day camp parents.
- ☀ Check the *yellow pages* of your local directory under day camps.
- ☀ Work with a *camp adviser*. These professionals help families find the right summer program for their child. The camp adviser generally doesn't charge the family a fee, but rather is paid by the camp for each referral made. Check in the yellow pages under Camp Adviser.
- ☀ Check *local preschools*. Many offer summer programs that are geared to the under-five set.
- ☀ Visit a *camp fair* where you will have an opportunity to talk to representatives from a wide range of programs.

Camps Come in All Shapes and Sizes

Your budget will obviously influence your choice of camp, but so too will your own assessment of what your child needs and can appreciate. Bigger is not always better, and maybe even not necessary depending on your child's age and personality, your budget, and your goals for the summer experience.

As one family of three sons, ages four, six, and ten years old, discovered, the needs and demands of each child may be met in three different programs. Here is their story which is illustrative of the variety of day camps available, with the advantages and disadvantages of each type.

For the four-year-old, the choices were: a camp sponsored by the *nursery school* the little boy was already attending; a program offered by the town *recreation department*; and a *private day camp*. The camp fees ranged from $175 for the recreational department program, which was five mornings a week for six weeks; $850 for the camp at the nursery school, which was also five mornings a week for six weeks; and $1,800 for the private camp program, which was five mornings a week for eight weeks, with the option of a longer day. Bus transportation was available, for a fee. (For older children, the day camp program ran from 9:00 to 4:00 and cost about $3,200 for an eight-week program.)

The *nursery school program* had the advantage of the well known. There would be no separation problems since the child was already familiar and comfortable with the school and teachers. The staff was clearly well trained in dealing with young children, and since this little boy was already a student at the school (as had his brothers been), there would be no learning curve about rules and preferences either by the youngster or the professionals in the first few days of camp. Plus several of his classmates would also be attending so he would already have some friends in his group.

On the other hand, since the little boy would be returning to the same preschool in the fall for the four-year-olds class, the parents were concerned whether, in fact, it was too much of a good thing. Should they choose a different environment for the summer months so it would be exciting to return to school in the fall? Moreover, the nursery school did not have a swimming pool, so the children could only play in sprinklers. There was no transportation available, so it meant setting up car pools for the summer.

The local *recreation program*, besides having the advantage of price, was also convenient. It was held at the elementary school, within walking distance of the family home. There was the added plus that neighborhood kids, who would be his classmates in kindergarten, would also be attending. It would be easy to arrange play dates and pickups at the end of the camp day. Furthermore, since the program was held in the kindergarten rooms, and used the kindergarten playground, the equipment was appropriately scaled to size—and it offered the little boy a nice introduction to the school he would be attending in another year.

But the counselors at the recreation camp were teenagers, although the supervisory staff were adults. As the youngest child, this little boy was fairly adaptable and would probably not have a separation problem. But again, there would be no water play, except for sprinklers, and activities would be limited to what could be played on the blacktop, since there was no field associated with the school.

The *private camp* offered many more activities, swimming twice a day, and the option of a longer day (for an additional fee). The campsite was large and beautiful, the equipment well maintained and appropriately sized, the counselors and specialists well trained and skilled at working with preschoolers.

However, the camp fees were more than double what even the nursery school program would be, and nine times the cost of the recreation program. Did the four-year-old need all those activities—although he really enjoyed the water and would benefit from swimming instruction? But if the family didn't use the camp bus, which involved a ride of close to an hour each way, it meant twice-a-day trips to the campsite for delivery and pickup.

The choices for the six-year-old were in some ways easier. The *recreation department* sponsored a program for children entering the first grade through sixth grade. It met five days a week, from 9:00 to 1:00 at the local park. The price was good and many kids in the town participated. For the six-year-old, it was a good way to meet the children from the other kindergarten classes, some of whom would be in his first-grade class. The park was within walking distance of home, and the program used the adjacent town pool for daily swim periods.

However, the program only ran until 1:00, which meant the six-year-old would be looking for a play date every afternoon. While the campers could swim in the town pool, the camp offered no swim lessons. This meant the family would have to schedule and pay for private swim lessons. Furthermore, the counselors were all teenagers, which was fun, but sometimes the supervision seemed somewhat lax since the teens tended to chat among themselves. The activities were limited to what could be played on the park's fields, and there were no specialists in any specific sports. The craft projects were uninspiring. If it rained, the camp would meet in the gymnasium of the nearby middle school, and the campers would watch videos or play pickup games.

The same *private day camp* program was available to the six-year-old with some of the same pluses and minuses. It was a full-day program for the six-year-old so there wouldn't be the hassle of trying to fit in play dates. The sports and activities offered were much more impressive. If it rained, the camp had 15 buildings so many of the activities could continue. And if necessary, the camp would take the kids to a local bowling alley or roller skating rink for an outing. Furthermore, for kids in third grade and above, there was, for an added fee, a sleepaway camp introduction. The children could spend a week at an established overnight camp—accompanied by their own day camp counselors. *But* the price for an eight-week program at the private day camp was significantly higher than the local recreation program and the long bus trip was still an issue.

Another option for the six-year-old, but in some ways more attractive to the ten-year-old, was piecing together a summer of *specialized camp programs*. The fifth grader, who had already attended a general interest day camp for three years, now wanted to spend two weeks at soccer camp, two weeks at baseball camp, and two weeks at computer camp. Each program cost about $300 a week. The day at each of these specialized camps was devoted primarily to lessons, drills, practices, games, and tournaments. It was learning and fun, but single focused. Would the boys be better off at a program that was more well rounded? The privately owned specialty camps were at different sites, with pickup and delivery from a central location. For the ten-year-old, the parents were also considering sleepaway camp options.

For this family, choosing the right camp for each child was a balancing act. There were issues of time, comfort, and a philosophical question of how to spend the summer. And there were, of course, budget considerations. One of the kids always seemed to be getting a cold, ear infection, stomach virus, etc. The local recreational program cost about $8 per day (less than a baby-sitter), so if a child missed a day, it wasn't too bad. On the other hand, a day at a private camp cost about $80, so a three-day stomach virus was expensive. However, the program at the private camp was a much broader, richer experience.

If there is a variety of camp choices in your community, how you choose the right one for your child will take time and effort. But a step-by-step approach will help you narrow the field considerably. Here's how.

WHEN TO START THE SEARCH?

Ideally, you should start your search *at least a full year* before you plan to enroll your child. That makes sense because it's the only way you can observe day camps while they're in session. Some parents worry that their child may change dramatically in 12 months and the choice they make today won't be right a year later. Others are concerned that the counselors they observe and think are just perfect won't be there next year.

Although these worries are legitimate, it is reassuring to know that while your child will undoubtedly mature over a year, you are looking, in the broad sense, for a basic philosophical match between your approach to kids and the day camp; for a caring, creative staff who clearly enjoy working with young children; for a safe, nurturing environment. Therefore, if it's a well-run program, in a clean, safe environment, with a caring, professional staff, then it will still be a good match a year later.

The search process helps you to focus on what you believe is important in a day camp program. It allows you time to see how different day camps handle similar problems. And allowing yourself enough time to search gives you the widest number of choices.

If you aren't able to visit the camp while it is in session, then you will have to rely on interviews with the director, brochures and videos, as well as conversations with camp-provided references to make your decision.

SCHEDULING THE VISIT

Should you take your child along when you visit camps? This is a matter of judgment. If your child is a preschooler, then it's probably better to visit the camp *without* your child. It's a scouting mission. You need time to observe and ask questions without distraction. But if your child is over

> **TIP: Check It Out**
> When you begin your search, use the day camp checklist (see Appendix 1) or keep your own journal so that you can review and compare your findings later.

> **TIP:**
> Allow at least an hour for each day camp. This will give you time to see the children move between several activities. You also want to talk to the camp director for at least 15 minutes.

five, take her along if possible. One indication of a good camp director is how she includes your child in the visit. She should make an effort to ask your youngster's opinions and preferences, and pay attention to questions. You want to see that the director, who sets the tone for the camp, respects and enjoys kids. Better that the director answers your child's questions, and if necessary, sets a time for a phone interview with you to address your concerns.

Call for an appointment to visit. It's unfair to expect the staff to show you the camp if you stop by unexpectedly.

But to save yourself time, you can get the answers to many of your basic questions from a phone call.

1. **How long has the camp been in business?** This gives you an idea of the stability and strength of the camp program.

2. **Who sponsors the camp?** Is it a privately owned business, sponsored by a nonprofit organization, affiliated with a religious institution, or run by the town or county?

3. **How many children attend the camp?** How many children are in the specific age group of your child? An even number of boys and girls? How are the groups organized? Can your child be placed with a friend?

4. **What is the ratio of counselors to children?** Especially for younger (preschool) children, you want to see a program that has small groups (one to six), or at least if the group is larger, additional counselors. You need that level of coverage to ensure a high quality and safe program. The American Camping Association has these standards for older campers:

Age	Counselor to Children Ratio
6 to 8 years old	1 counselor per 8 campers
9 to 14 years old	1 counselor for every 10 campers
15 to 18 years old	1 counselor for every 12 campers

5. **Is the camp accredited? By whom?** The American Camping Association, an independent organization, accredits summer camps based on nationally accepted standards for health, safety, and program quality. Accreditation is a voluntary process by which camps are evaluated every three years on nearly 300 standards affecting health and safety, camp management, personnel, programming, and facilities. However, only about 25 percent of day camps choose to undergo the lengthy accreditation process. It's a good indication of a program's commitment to high standards if it has undergone the process. And even if a camp has been accredited by the ACA, you still need to make sure it's the right program for your child, as well as do the usual reference check.

Licensing by appropriate state and local authorities is an absolute requirement. Check with your local health department to see if the camps you are visiting are licensed. It is no guarantee of excellence, but it at least ensures compliance with minimum health and safety requirements.

6. **Does the camp provide any marketing materials?** Ask if the camp has any brochures, pamphlets, or videos describing the program. If so, ask to have them mailed to you so you can review them before your visit. You will want to see if reality matches the description. You may discover that the program emphasizes activities which are of no interest to you, and save yourself a trip.

NARROWING THE FIELD FURTHER

Once you've made a list of possible options, you need to determine those camps that meet your criteria for excellence. Here are important issues you must consider when evaluating camps.

Location

Where the camp is located may or may not be important to you. Some parents prefer that the camp is near home, especially if their children are young, even if they live in the city and it limits the kind of program the camp can provide. For others, they deliberately want a suburban or rural location as a contrast to their urban living. Some parents want the day camp located near their place of work rather than near home. One family who commutes to work an hour each way, deliberately chose a day camp near the place of the parents' employment so that the family could commute together.

There are advantages and disadvantages to each choice.

Near Home A camp that is within a short car ride to your home generally means less rushing in the morning. If you need only allow 10 minutes to get to camp, it may lessen the morning crazies. Especially if that is an issue during the school year, you may prefer to have more relaxed summer mornings. It will also mean that your child is likely to see familiar faces at camp from your community, which may make the transition easier.

Near Work Some parents choose a camp near their jobs in order to be close in case of an emergency. They also enjoy the additional time they can spend with their child during the commute. This alternative works best if after-camp child care is also located nearby.

Near Child Care You may prefer to choose a camp that is located conveniently for your baby-sitter. One family opted to put their son in a day camp located near their sitter. The family arranged a car pool where the parents drove in the morning, and the other members of the car pool picked up at the end of the camp day and delivered the child to the sitter.

At a Distance Some parents are so committed to a certain camp program that they are willing to go outside of their community or drive a distance in order for their child to participate. If they live in a city, they may want their child to attend a camp in a suburban or rural environment. It may be worth it, but keep in mind that it will lengthen the day when you factor in the commute.

STAFF

The essence of any good program is the staff. You want to know:

1. **The credentials of the director, counselors, specialists, and staff.**
   For the preschooler, at least the head counselor of the group should be a preschool teacher or trained in early childhood education. Even *for the older child*, you are looking for a staff that is mature and expe-

rienced, who clearly enjoy being around kids. The camp's *senior staff* should be adults with experience in running a camp and working with children.

The *specialists* who teach activities and skills must be, not only proficient in the area of expertise, but also experienced in teaching children. Ask about the specialists' credentials in the field, but you want to see they have hands-on experience with children as well.

2. **Who on the staff is certified in lifesaving techniques (CPR)?**

Preferably, several members of the staff have this training.

3. **How does the camp screen its staff?**

You want to know that the camp takes active steps to check references. You want to make sure that the counselors and support staff are individuals without any kind of criminal record, who are safe to be around young children.

4. **How many of the staff are returning from the previous year? How many of the staff are former campers?**

It's a sign of a good program if a majority of the staff return year after year. However, many camp counselors "age out," as they get older and need to seek year-round or more lucrative employment. Similarly, it speaks well of the program if former campers choose to return as counselors.

5. **How long has the director been in the position? Is he the owner as well? If not, who is?**

The director of the day camp sets the tone for the program. In addition to being responsible for a myriad of administrative details, generally he hires and supervises the staff. The director should believe in and be able to articulate the camp's philosophy. When necessary he serves as a buffer between parents and staff.

CHECK IT OUT

When you visit the camp, you'll want to notice:

1. How do the counselors handle transitions? Many youngsters have trouble moving from one activity to another—from arts and crafts to

swimming; from gymnastics to kickball. How well a counselor can handle a child's natural reluctance to move on from a fun activity is a good barometer of how she handles difficult situations. Kids dawdle—how does the counselor keep the group together?

2. Do the counselors respect campers? Counselors should never ridicule or make a child the butt of the joke. They play a critical role in building a child's self-esteem as he tries new experiences. Nurturing, thoughtful, fair, and perhaps the most essential ingredient—a sense of humor—are all critical qualities in a counselor. Watch how the counselors interact with the campers.

3. Does the counselor need to raise her voice frequently, either in anger or to get the children's attention? If a counselor has to raise her voice often it may mean that she doesn't have control of her group. The kids are excited and having fun, so it may be difficult to get their attention—what techniques does the counselor use?

4. How does the counselor handle aggression among the children? How does she handle a situation calling for discipline? In day camps, a good counselor heads off potential problems, keeping an eye on situations that may possibly be heading for danger, distracting a youngster she sees heading down a road she knows is trouble or avoiding situations, such as pairing a mischievous twosome, which can only be a problem.

5. When observing a day camp group, you should see counselors and specialists giving frequent, positive reinforcement.

Gender Equity

When you observe a day camp, you want to be sure that both boys and girls have *equal access to and encouragement to try* all the activity areas. Childhood is a critical time for the development of a child's self-image as a competent individual. You don't want a program that limits a child in any way—especially based on gender.

1. Are girls encouraged to try (and excel) in traditionally male activities, such as all sports areas, crafts, such as woodworking?

2. Do boys participate in all crafts areas, including jewelry making and macrame—traditionally female activities?

Staff Specialists

Many camps hire a myriad of specialists to enrich their program. Check:

* ☼ the credentials of the specialists the camp uses
* ☼ how often classes are held
* ☼ how the camp handles children who don't want to participate
* ☼ how well the specialists relate to the children
* ☼ whether they are able to communicate effectively. Are they fluent in English?
* ☼ what do the group counselors do while the campers are in a specialty activity? Are the counselors expected to accompany the campers, participate in the activity, assist?

The Children

You are not only observing the counselors when you visit a day camp, you also want to watch the children. They are the best indication if the program is working.

* ☼ Do the children seem happy? You can see it in their faces. Are they busy, engaged in their activities?
* ☼ Can you sense an underlying excitement?
* ☼ If the group is noisy, are they under control? Children may be talking to one another, even cheering, but you can sense when the situation is out of control. Do the children seem to be interacting well with each other?
* ☼ Are there any children who seem isolated? What do the counselors do to integrate them into the group?
* ☼ How diverse are the campers? Is that important to you? Is there a relatively even number of boys and girls?
* ☼ If you will not be enrolling your child in camp at the beginning of the season, for example, she is enrolling two weeks after the season begins, ask how the camp integrates a new camper into a group that has been together for several weeks.

MEDICAL CARE

Kids get sick at camp and some may get hurt, even under strong supervision.

☀ Is there a full-time nurse on the staff?

☀ Are medical exams required? Are immunizations required? The answer should be *yes* to both questions.

☀ Does the nurse check the campers for head lice? No one likes to talk about this problem, but it's a serious issue for all camps, and no reflection on the cleanliness of the facilities. Checking for head lice at the beginning of the season cuts down on the problem. Notifying families when there is an outbreak also helps.

☀ Is the nurse qualified to dispense medication (with proper authorization)?

☀ What is the camp policy in the event of a medical emergency? Is there a designated hospital and how far away is it? What kind of transportation is used?

☀ Lyme disease is a tick-borne disease. It occurs most commonly in wooded areas in the East and parts of the Midwest. If you live in an affected area, ask the director about the incidence of cases among campers.

☀ Are counselors trained to handle minor medical emergencies, e.g., bumps, bruises, scrapes, and cuts?

☀ What are the camp rules for keeping a sick child home? For example, while everyone would agree that a child with a temperature does not belong in camp, what about runny noses?

ACTIVITIES

Space and cost considerations affect the number and variety of activities a camp will offer. Ask to see a sample of a typical camp day (see the following sample schedule from a private day camp, as well as for a recreation program sponsored by a town).

While swimming lessons are given every day, other activities scheduled during the day may include karate, science, music, drama, clay, computers, and creative movement.

At some camps the choice of activities is nothing short of dazzling. You want to know:

☀ Are all the activities open to all age groups?

☀ How often can a child take a certain activity? Daily? For the entire summer?

SCHEDULE FOR PRIVATE DAY CAMP
(FOR SEVEN-YEAR-OLDS)

9:00—9:15	Campers arrive, morning meeting
9:15—10:15	Swim and change
10:15—11:00	Arts and Crafts
11:00—11:30	Nature
11:30—12:30	Lunch
12:30—1:30	Sports
1:30—2:00	Jewelry making
2:15—3:00	Gymnastics
3:00—3:30	Playground
3:30—4:00	Snack
4:00	Dismissal

SCHEDULE FOR CAMP SPONSORED
BY TOWN RECREATION DEPARTMENT

9:00—9:15	Meet at flagpole, announcements
9:15—10:15	First activity/arts and crafts
10:30—11:15	Swimming
11:30—11:45	Snack
12:00—12:50	Second activity/if arts and crafts in morning, then sports/games in afternoon
1:00	Dismissal

☼ Does the camp insist that all campers try all activities?

☼ Are there different levels of expertise in sports? If so, how are teams chosen?

☼ Are there any inter-camp (with other camps) competitions?

☼ Are the activities sufficiently challenging as the camper gets older? If the camp has a program for both younger and older children, is there room to grow? Will the older camper be bored if she has attended the program for several years—or is there always something new to try?

Here is a list of some of the typical activities found at day camps. The larger private camps may offer more of these activities than you'll find at a program sponsored by a nonprofit organization or town recreation program.

Sports: soccer, baseball, softball, basketball, kickball, dodgeball, track, field hockey, aerobics, gymnastics, volleyball, tennis, martial arts, platform tennis, swimming, miniature golf, archery

Arts and Crafts: clay, woodworking, paints, papier-mâché, origami, tie-dying, macrame

Other Activities: dance, nature study, computer, theater

Waterfront: swimming, diving, canoeing, sailing, power boating, water skiing, scuba diving

FACILITIES

How big is the camp in acreage? What kind of a waterfront does it offer? Is there a stage for productions? pottery and jewelry-making building? zip line and/or climbing wall? roller hockey rink? Specifically you want to know:

The Outdoor Facilities

Part of every day camp program should include lots of opportunities for campers to exercise their large motor muscles. For preschoolers, a good day camp should have an appropriate playground.

Here's what to look for:

☀ Playgrounds should have at least 75 square feet per child.
☀ The surface under the equipment should be impact absorbing. Look for a play area that is built over *properly maintained* loose-filled material such as wood mulch, pea gravel, or sand. In order to be impact absorbing, the materials should be at least 9 to 12 inches deep (so these materials need to be replenished over time). Synthetic, foamlike tiles or rubber mats made especially for playground use are also safe.
☀ For preschoolers, the equipment should be scaled down for safety. Equipment should be no more than 5 feet high. There should be a protective surface below and a 6- to 8-foot perimeter surrounding the equipment so that a child can descend safely without falling onto

another child or structure. Any platform or walkway more than 20 inches above the ground should have guardrails or protective barriers.

☀ The equipment should be well maintained. Run your fingers over wooden climbing structures and check for splinters and look for loose screws.

☀ Is the sandbox covered after use to avoid animal droppings?

Grounds

☀ Are the playing fields level and free of rocks and debris?

☀ Are the playing fields freshly reseeded and kept? mowed?

The Pool

Water safety, if not the number one camp concern, should be ranked close to the top of the list. Look for:

☀ An experienced waterfront staff committed to safety first. Ask for the credentials of the pool and/or waterfront staff. Swimming teachers should have Red Cross lifesaving certification.

☀ Children should be tested for swimming skill level in the very beginning of camp. They should be tested again during the season to assess progress. If swimming lessons are offered, then specific Red Cross skill goals should be set for each camper.

☀ Nonswimmers must be clearly identified to lifeguards. Some camps insist that nonswimmers wear water wings or inflatable preservers during free swim; others believe that these water aids give a child a false sense of security. Whatever the policy, swimmers should only be allowed to be in the water depth that is appropriate for their skill level (for example, nonswimmers would remain in the shallow end of the pool where the water depth is no more than 3 feet).

☀ The pool should be large enough to accommodate the campers so the children can swim easily without bumping into one another.

☀ If there is only one pool, there should be different depth levels to meet the needs of varying skill levels. Ideally, there would be a separate pool for preschoolers, with a depth of less than 3 feet).

☀ There should be clearly marked, separate areas for swimming, boating, water skiing, and diving.

☀ There should be an established water "buddy" policy for all swimming sessions. Children should be drilled in water safety.

☼ In addition to lifeguards, there should be counselors *in the water* and on deck to supervise during free swim.

☼ If there is boating, sailing, and water skiing, campers should always wear life jackets when engaged in these water sports.

FOOD

Some camps provide both lunch and snacks; at others, campers bring their own. You'll want to know:

1. What is the typical menu? Do children have any choice? Is a favorite staple like peanut butter always available as a substitute?

2. What are the snacks and when are they offered?

3. If campers bring their own lunches, are they refrigerated to avoid spoilage?

ARTS AND CRAFTS

Most former campers remember the craft projects they brought home. The arts and crafts program at a day camp gives a remarkably clear insight into the camp's general philosophy. Is the camp interested in the product or the process? Are the projects individualistic or cookie-cutter duplicates? It's fine to have some projects where every child uses similar things, for example, decorating a frame with a variety of materials from nature. But each child should be able to choose which and how much of the materials to use.

☼ Ask to see typical craft projects. What is the range of crafts, pottery, woodworking, macrame, jewelry making?

☼ Are there enough supplies so that more than one camper can participate in an activity at the same time? For example, is there more than one pottery wheel?

Indoor Alternatives

While you would hope for a summer full of sunny days, rain happens. So what's the plan? There should be a large indoor space where kids can play. Make sure it is well maintained, well lit, and well ventilated.

But the director should also tell you about alternative plans for inclement weather. One director recalled a summer where it rained 29 out of 40 days! You don't want to think that your child is spending all that time watching videos.

Ask for a worst case scenario from the director. Besides the facilities at the camp for rainy day activities, does the director bring in outside entertainment, such as magicians, science fun, jugglers?

The Campsite

Is it well maintained, easily walkable, and is there shade as well as fields?

Safety First

The camp should have clear policies that protect the safety of the children. You want to know about:

ARRIVAL/DISMISSAL

What are the arrival/dismissal plans for the camp? Children should be safely and properly supervised by the staff where they are dropped off and picked up. There are many ways to handle these potentially dangerous situations. Some camps insist that all cars park in a lot away from the camp and parents/caregivers then walk over and pick up their child/car pool. Others have a drive-through procedure where the cars line up and then each child (and her car-pool mates) is placed into the car by the staff.

Bus Travel Rules

Forty years later, one dad recounts the story of his own first day on the bus. He remembers standing on the corner waiting with a dozen other kids in his neighborhood. He scrambled up the bus steps, grabbed a seat, and only when the bus rumbled off, did he notice that his T-shirt wasn't the same color as everyone else's. He walked up to the bus driver and asked, "Is this the bus for Camp Simon?" The bus driver looked at the little boy and asked, "Aren't you Harriet Levine?"

While this dad can now laugh heartily when recounting his tale of the opening day of camp, you need to know that your child will be safe on the camp bus. If you opt for a camp that provides transportation, check it out.

☼ What kind of cars, vans, or buses does the camp use?
☼ How are the vehicles marked (so a child can readily tell if it is his camp bus or not)?

☼ Ask about the safety and organizational rules the camp has in place to make sure that the campers board the right bus, both for the ride to camp and for the ride home in the evening.

☼ Question what kind of safety procedures are followed to make sure that the camper is safe once she disembarks the bus: Are there flags to stop traffic? Does a counselor accompany the camper to the door? Will the camper have to cross the street? Is it door-to-door delivery or pick up/delivery at a central location?

☼ Is there a counselor on board as well as the driver—there should be.

☼ How long is the trip including all the pickups?

☼ Will the bus bring children home who are on another bus route for play dates (with permission/authorization of course)?

☼ Are there seat belts for each child and does the bus counselor monitor that children wear them?

☼ Can you send in a list of authorized persons who can pick up your child at the bus stop?

☼ How long will the bus driver wait in the morning before leaving (should you be running late)?

☼ Does the camp send the bus and monitors on a pre-camp trial run so that the campers can meet them before the season begins?

For the Urban Camp

If the camp is located in an urban area where children walk to camp or use public transportation, what are the strategies for ensuring a safe transference from caregiver to staff, and then the reverse at the end of the day? Does the camp's plan seem safe and appropriate for its location?

Camp Security

While the camp should have an open-door policy for parents that permits you to visit and, when appropriate, participate, the camp should also have a clear procedure to screen visitors and keep out strangers. Basic safety precautions should also be clearly in evidence.

☼ Do all visitors have to check in at the main office? Does each visitor wear an identifying badge?

☼ Is there a procedure in place to admit/screen visitors?

☼ Are there working fire alarms and fire extinguishers in each building? Are there emergency lights, and is there a posted emergency exit plan?

☀ Does the camp hold fire drills with the children?
☀ Can all buildings be easily evacuated?

LET'S TALK ABOUT $$$

An important consideration in choosing a day camp is whether or not you can afford it. Scholarships are generally limited, although camps sponsored by nonprofit associations are more likely to have some form of assistance.

☀ Ask for a breakdown of the fees: Does it include transportation, lunch, uniforms/T-shirts? Do you need to buy additional uniforms/T-shirts?
☀ Often there is a break in the price if you enroll your child for the entire summer, rather than for just two, four, or six weeks. One family discovered that although their daughter would miss the first week of camp because of a family vacation, it was still cheaper to pay for the entire summer, rather than per week.
☀ Ask if there is a family discount if you enroll siblings in the program.
☀ If you are only interested in a four-week program, you may find that some day camps offer a reduced fee for the last four weeks of camp (rather than the first four) because many families leave in August for vacation.

Camp fees vary enormously across the country and among the different types of camps. Two important points:

1. More expensive does not necessarily mean better.
2. But if a camp is considerably cheaper than others in the same area, you will want to know where they are cutting costs.

CHECK IT OUT

Once you've selected a camp program, check references. Ask the director to give you the names of several families who have children enrolled in the program. Call and ask:

☀ their opinion of the camp program and personnel
☀ any problems their child encountered

☼ any staff member who was either outstanding or a problem

☼ how the director handled any issues that developed during the season

☼ if your child is using camp-provided transportation, ask for an evaluation of the personnel and vehicles

Check with the Better Business Bureau for any complaints about the camp.

Check with your pediatrician for his opinion of the program and if it seems appropriate for your child.

THE OPENING DAYS OF CAMP

If your child has not previously seen the camp, be sure and visit before camp begins. Just walking around the camp and getting a feel for the site, will make the opening day of camp a little easier.

Similarly, if your child has never taken a bus before, and will be riding a bus to camp for the first time, ask to see the bus and even let her board it. Many camps arrange a visit by the bus and staff before the program begins so the camper can familiarize himself with the driver's and counselors' faces and the vehicle.

On the opening day, wait with your child for the bus and make sure he is settled and buckled in. Wave and smile as the bus rides away. There may be a few tears, for the very young camper, but assure him that you will be waiting for his return in a few hours. For your own peace of mind, call the camp in a few hours to check on your child's adjustment.

If you are taking your child to camp on opening day, make a direct handoff to a counselor. Don't send him over to a group of children, but introduce yourself and your child to the counselor before departing.

See Appendix 5 for a suggested reading list. Many of these books will convince your child that day camp is a fun place to be. Read a few with your child before summer begins.

THERE'S A PROBLEM

Don't hesitate to call the camp director if there is a problem at camp—or at home. The more information the camp has, the easier it will be for them to help your child.

For example, if there is a new baby at home, a grandparent is ill, parents are going on vacation without the kids—let the camp know. Your child may have difficulty adjusting to the situation at home, and evidencing it in behavior at camp. Help put it in context for the camp so they can help your youngster.

On the other hand, if there is a problem at camp, don't hesitate to notify the counselors and if necessary, the director. After several days of teasing by two fellow campers, one little girl was reluctant to return to camp. A conversation with the group leader ended the problem—quickly. The only regret, says the mother, was she should have spoken sooner. (On the other hand, it is reasonable, especially for older campers, to see if they can resolve the dispute themselves, at least at first.)

If your child is having a problem with a counselor or specialist, call the director. Explain, without rancor, what the problem is and how long it has been going on. Ask the director to investigate and report back to you. Agree to talk again to see if the problem has been satisfactorily resolved.

CONVERSATIONS AT HOME

Once camp's begun, you'll want your child to share the fun and excitement with you. There's time enough in the teen years for monosyllabic answers to the parental question: "What did you do today?" Learning to share with each other the daily activities of your day reinforces the parent-child relationship. You are genuinely interested in what your child did, and you want to hear the good parts, as well as the bad.

But a child's reticence is a combination of factors.

☼ **Out of sight, out of mind** Often kids just don't keep the memory of the day's events clear and in focus. It's not that it wasn't fun or that it was so boring it wasn't worth remembering.

☼ **Here and now** Children tend to focus on the here and now, rather than the past. *What are we having for dinner? May I watch television or play a video game?* Those are their immediate concerns.

☼ **Language skills may be limited** Some kids are very articulate, while others still have difficulty organizing and expressing their thoughts—but practice does make a difference.

☼ **Too much to tell** Sometimes, the day was so full of activities, that it's hard for your child to single out one activity and talk about it. Or they are so overwhelmed by how much they have to tell you, that the words come tumbling out incoherently.

☀ **Processing what's happening** Sometimes young children (and adults too) need time to understand and incorporate an experience before they can talk about it. Don't be surprised if your child waits a day or even a few weeks before he talks about certain events. He needs the time to figure out what the experience means to him and how to talk about it.

Here are some tips to make the conversations smoother.

☀ **Understand the basics** It helps if you understand the normal schedule so you can ask specific questions, which helps your child focus, for example, "What did you do during arts and crafts today."

☀ **Set the stage** It helps to have a block of uninterrupted time to talk about what's happening in your child's life. Turn off the television and put on the telephone answering machine. Snuggle down on the couch for a chat. It doesn't have to be too long—15 minutes is fine—but it tells your child that you are interested enough in his life to focus on him exclusively for a period of time.

☀ **Work together** Other parents find that doing a chore together with their child sparks conversation. As you wash the dishes and clean up after dinner, your child may feel that the focus is less intense and the conversation easier.

☀ **Riding in the car** When you are alone in the car is another great chance for some quality one-on-one conversation.

☀ **Be specific** It helps your child focus if you ask precise questions. For example, you could begin with "Who did you sit with on the bus today?"

☀ **Get to know the other kids** Take the time to put the faces to the names your child is mentioning. Then you'll know whom she is referring to when she answers your questions and you can keep the conversation going more easily.

☀ **Wait for an answer** Don't be uncomfortable with silence. It may take your child a few moments to organize her thoughts about the day. Allowing time for her to answer your question helps develop her language skills as well.

☀ **Model it** Talk to your child about *your* day. This shows her that discussing the day's events are part of your family's life.

DO KIDS NEED PRIVACY?

You want your child to respect your privacy, and you must respect your child's need for privacy as well. If your child appears happy in camp, does not exhibit any problems with sleeping, eating, socializing, etc., then you need to respect his willingness (and ability) to share his day with you on his terms. That may mean that some days he will be full of answers to the question: What happened at camp today—and sometimes he'll respond with the classic "same old stuff" and nothing more.

Put the child and the situation in perspective. Some kids are chatterboxes and tell all (sometimes more than you even want to know!), while others are "silent Sams." *What's important is that your child feels she can talk to you when she needs to.*

Your child may enjoy the day camp experience so much that she wants to return year after year. Or she may be interested in trying sleepaway camp, a specialty camp, or a special program for teens. In the chapters ahead we'll explore some of the alternatives, but they don't detract from the richness of a good day camp experience. Day camps can be an exciting introduction to camp life and the source of a lifetime of memories.

Chapter **2**

SLEEPAWAY CAMPS:
FUN PLUS

I talk to her almost every day. We met at camp when we were seven years old, so it's now almost 50 years we've been friends. We didn't live in the same town, but kept in touch from one camp season to the next. When things weren't going well with my friends at home, I knew I always could call her up and hear a friendly voice. We went to each other's weddings, watched each other's kids grow up. Now we're starting on the grandchildren together. There's something special about camp friendships. Maybe it's because you're a bunch of kids living together, and even though there is plenty of supervision, you feel like you're on your own. It's a chance to try your wings, but with a safety net that's there to catch you if you fall.

Unlike school, you don't have to go to summer camp—and you certainly don't have to attend sleepaway camp. It's an option—but one that, despite the costs, attracts more than 5 million kids each year.

The process of choosing the right overnight camp for your child begins months before the first day of summer. In fact, some of the decisions you will make have less to do with any one specific camp and more about the needs of, and the kind of camp you want for, your child.

> **TIP:**
>
> Choosing a camp is a personal decision—one that has to be a good match for your child, and for you. You should make your decision after thinking about your own family's lifestyle, and trying to match your child's personality and needs to the programs that you have seen.

✶ General interest or specialty camp?
✶ Private or nonprofit camp?
✶ Affiliated with a church/synagogue or secular?
✶ Full summer program or four weeks, two weeks, one week?

There are, of course, certain standards, like those that have to do with safety or counselor/camper ratio, on which you should not compromise. But there are many other issues which are a matter of personal choice, for which you, the parent, will have to decide what is best for your child, what you feel is essential, what can be compromised. During the process of reading about camps, you should develop a checklist of those qualities that you want in a camp. You should prioritize them so that the program you select for your child will meet at least the most important of the standards on your list.

It's possible that, after much thought, you decide that the quality of a specific program is so outstanding that you are willing to put aside certain criteria. For example, while you might prefer to send your child to a religiously affiliated camp, you discover a secular program is a better match. Or you might find that although you and a friend with a child of the same age are trying to choose a camp for both children, a certain program will be perfect for one child, and not as good a fit for the other.

You want to select a camp that is compatible with your own child-rearing philosophy *and* your child's needs. This is important because a basic compatibility between camp and home will avoid confusing your child, reduce unreasonable parental expectations, and facilitate parent-camp communication. You want your child to hear the same messages at home and at camp.

WHAT DOES A CHILD LEARN AT SLEEPAWAY CAMP?

Camp can be every bit as educational as school, without the desks and homework. Within the context of play, children learn a wide range of skills and develop physically, emotionally, socially, and intellectually. Camp gives kids an opportunity to learn the way children learn best: *by doing, living, experiencing* it for themselves. This method of learning is based on theories developed by Jean Piaget, a Swiss psychologist (1896–1980). But it's an educational philosophy that parents have always understood. It's one thing to read about nature in a book or watch a nature program on television. But you *experience* the forces of nature when you hike the hills, swim in the rivers, witness the magic of a star-filled night.

There's another dynamic that happens at camp. Often kids are more willing to take risks and try new activities because they *choose* to do so. It's a voluntary decision, unlike the compulsory requirements of school. With no grades, just personal satisfaction as the motivating factor, children are frequently more open to new experiences.

Add to the mix that camp offers a wide variety of arenas in which to excel. At a good general interest camp, the *nonathlete* has opportunities to shine in the woodworking shop, the camp musicals, or arts and crafts, while still enjoying the benefits of a strong physical program. The *athlete* too can find dozens of outlets for his skills, but also has the opportunity to tap into other sides of his personality. And the two campers, perhaps diametrically opposite in interests, learn to live together, which is perhaps the most valuable camp skill of all.

Opportunities = Competence = Enhanced Self-Esteem

Camp offers kids many different opportunities to become competent. To begin, youngsters have the chance to *practice* new (and old) skills on a regular, perhaps even daily, basis. Of course you'll see improvement! For the beginner swimmer, taking a lesson every day will undoubtedly make her a better swimmer by the end of camp. The novice has a chance to learn; the more experienced camper has an opportunity to improve.

Competence breeds self-esteem. She becomes more independent and self-reliant. In fact, while camp can be wonderful for all children, the child who is not strong academically can often find the supportive environment and a variety of activities in which she can shine.

Not the Same Old, Same Old

There's another benefit to sending your child to camp. It's an opportunity to try something new. Especially at general interest camps, youngsters are exposed to a range of experiences outside of their normal lives. No matter how many after-school clubs or lessons they take, it's unlikely they will have had the opportunity to learn or try all that a camp has to offer.

And in a supportive environment, the child may be willing to try—and possibly fail—at something new. The artist can play sports; the athlete can join the chorus.

And there is an interesting twist to these new opportunities. As one camper explained: "Because I didn't know anyone at the camp before I went, I felt a kind of freedom that I don't feel at home. Since no one *knew* me, I could try out for the camp play—even though back home I *never* participate in the school plays. In school, everyone thinks I'm a jock."

Furthermore, youngsters learn to set their own goals. One nine-year-old, a middling swimmer when camp began, was determined to be able to swim to the raft and back before the season was over, a 1-mile round trip. Only a select group of campers pass this milestone each year. Every day he practiced and his stroke got stronger as the weeks passed. The sense of personal triumph and accomplishment this camper experienced when, in the last week of camp, he did swim to the raft and back was remarkable and would have a profound effect on this child's self-esteem.

Failure Isn't a Dirty Word

Finally, the camp program encourages children to test themselves, to risk failure, knowing that a nonjudgmental, encouraging community will support the choice. *The child learns that failing is not a problem—failing to take a risk is.* There are no grades at camp and certainly your future (or choice of college and career) doesn't depend on what you do at camp. In fact, the best thing a parent can advise a child setting off for camp for the first time is to "sample the menu of activities—you never know what you may like."

LIFE SKILLS TAUGHT HERE

Your child may not remember, even one year later, how to play capture the flag or the songs from color war, but she will recall the life lessons that she learned at camp and these will stand her in good stead through adulthood.

Your camper will learn to take responsibility for herself, her belongings, even to some extent, her health. There's no maid service at camp, so even the youngster who has never made a bed before, will learn how to make hospital corners and roll a blanket. The camper will be responsible for keeping the area around her bunk neat, her belongings returned to the assigned cubby. This personal sense of responsibility fosters independence and builds self-esteem.

Although counselors are there to remind and encourage, the camper must take responsibility for her personal hygiene. If a camper doesn't learn quickly the need for showers, tooth brushing, and shampooing, certainly her bunkmates will remind her! But once learned, the child takes an important step toward maturity and independence.

Another important life lesson from a summer at camp is learning to take responsibility for your own health. The counselors and director have responsibility to take charge in case of emergency or serious illness, but for daily discomforts, mild sniffles, poison ivy, the camper discovers how to articulate what hurts and to seek help.

Finally, one of the most important benefits of camp is learning how to get along with others. Living together 24 hours a day teaches children about compromise, teamwork, respect for others, and courtesy.

Camp also improves a child's social skills. It's an opportunity to make new friends. Learning how to reach out and develop a friendship with a stranger is an important life lesson.

THE HIDDEN BENEFITS OF CAMP

Overnight camp can offer a child summers to remember and cherish, but parents too enjoy benefits.

There is the relief of knowing that your child is in a safe, exciting environment throughout the long, summer days (and nights). Child care is always an issue when both parents work outside the home. At least for the length of the camp session, you are relieved of the daily decision about child care. Even if child care isn't an issue, finding suitable activities during the summer (and television shouldn't be one of them!) can often be difficult. But even more problematic is finding peers. Often neighborhoods empty out during the summer as kids go to camp, families go on vacations. Even if you are able to "entertain" your child during the summer, he will be looking for other kids with whom to play. Camp offers entertainment and constant peer company.

But let's be honest. Camp offers parents their own vacation. As one set of parents admitted (echoed by similar stories by dozens of other families), "The first year our daughter went to camp, we were at a loss, not quite knowing what to do with all our free time. Our family life revolved around our daughter who's an only child. But then after a few weeks, we began to rediscover what it was that we liked about each other, just like before we had a child. We miss our daughter, but frankly we have wonderful times during those eight weeks she is at camp. We eat what we want, when we want. We take trips for which she would have zero interest. And it's all guilt free because she has made it clear how much she loves camp."

For those families who have more than one child, it's interesting to see how the younger siblings shine during the older one's absence. One father pointed out how his younger daughter certainly missed her big sister, but was "reveling in being the center of attention for a change."

IS YOUR CHILD READY FOR CAMP?

Given the benefits of sleepaway camp, should all children enroll? Basically, yes. There are camps for almost all youngsters including those with special needs (see chapter 6). But are there exceptions to the rule? Are there some children who shouldn't go to camp?

Certainly there are youngsters who aren't *ready* for an overnight camp experience. Some may not be mature enough to handle the separation from home. Some camps accept children as young as six, but most child development experts suggest that a child should be at least eight years old before enrolling. One of the advantages of waiting is that the child can read and write. Letters from home, a source of comfort for the camper, can now be easily read by the child (see chapter 4 for how to stay in touch). Furthermore, the camper can personally write what's happening at camp (a source of comfort for the parents).

But, as parents know, chronological age isn't the definitive marker of readiness. Some youngsters are more than ready at six or seven years of age, especially younger siblings who can't wait finally to be at the camp of an older sibling. And there are eight-year-olds who need another year or two to be ready to handle the separation and independence. *Parents need to consider their child and his own readiness.* Here are some guidelines:

MY CHILD IS A BED WETTER

It's estimated that over five million school-age children in the United States suffer from enuresis (bed wetting). Families know the toll that this problem can take on a child's self-esteem, but is it a reason to avoid sleepaway camp?

Jennifer Millman, a private camp adviser with Student Camp and Trip Advisors in Fairfield, Connecticut, suggests that parents be honest and direct with camp directors when searching for a program. "Some camps are very experienced with this problem and go out of their way to make sure that the child never feels embarrassed. For example, at one camp I visited, each morning after the children went to breakfast, the counselor surreptitiously went back into the bunk and personally changed the sheets of the bed wetter so no one ever knew of the problem."

Ask the director for *specifics*. How does he train his staff to handle the problem on a daily basis (since they are the ones who are actually confronting and coping with the bed-wetting in the bunk). You want to know that, not only is the director sympathetic, but that he has in place a training program for his staff for how to deal with this sensitive issue.

Since children frequently outgrow bed-wetting, it may be easier to wait an extra year or two before sending a young (seven- or eight-year-old child) off to camp. The problem may resolve itself.

1. **Has your child enjoyed other overnight experiences?**

   Many children eagerly sleep over at friends' houses or grandparents' homes. This is a sign of readiness. If your child has been successful at spending the night away from you, it's an indication that he can function independently. If, on the other hand, you've gotten middle-of-the-night phone calls and had to rescue him from an overnight stay with a friend, it may be an indication that he's not quite ready for overnight camp.

2. **Has your child had other camp experiences?**

   It's helpful if a child has attended day camp prior to going to sleepaway camp for the first time. From a day camp program, a child learns to move from one activity to another, to make new friends, and develops cooperative and teamwork skills.

3. Is your child adaptable?

Going to overnight camp requires a certain degree of flexibility, an ability to adjust to new situations, and a willingness to try something new. Camp adjustment will be more difficult for the child who is fairly rigid and has difficulty in new situations. Of course, there is a period of adjustment for all kids. It's a rare child who is completely game for any new experience—but again, parents have a good idea of how well their child does when confronting unknown situations.

READY, SET, GO

Having decided that your child is ready for an overnight camp experience, there are still several issues you need to resolve before calling for the first brochure. In the process, you'll begin to narrow down the number of camps in your search process.

Time and Distance Requirements

Are there any geographical limitations to your search?

There's a big, wide world out there and lots of camps from which to choose. In fact, some parents opt to send their children to camps overseas as a way of adding another dimension to the experience. Your family needs to decide how close to home the camp must be.

If you choose a camp close to home, you eliminate some problems, face others; choosing a camp at a distance also has benefits and drawbacks.

CLOSE TO HOME

☼ **Travel to and from camp is simpler** Most camps provide transportation to and from camp, usually via buses. Choosing a camp close to home eliminates long bus rides and the accompanying motion sickness (which can be a miserable way to begin a camp experience).

☼ **Lower Costs** You reduce the expense of visiting your child at camp if you can make the visit and return home in the same day (rather than booking a room at a local motel). Furthermore, you lower the overall camp costs by eliminating or cutting travel costs for your camper.

☼ **Peace of Mind** There is a comfort in knowing that you can reach your child easily in case of emergency.

☼ **Familiar Faces** Your camper is more likely to bunk with kids from your general region, which may ease the transition. Friendships developed at camp are simpler to maintain during the rest of the year if the kids can easily meet and visit each other.

AT A DISTANCE

On the other hand, in many programs, the campers come from a wide geographic area and the diversity adds to the richness of the experience. Many camps are accustomed to making long-distance travel arrangements. Often the camper will fly, alone or with other campers from his area, into an airport close to the camp. There they will be met by camp officials and taken to camp, sometimes on the same bus with local campers.

But travel plans must take into account the age and maturity of the camper. One family was appalled when the camp director made reservations on an airline that required travelers to pay on board and in cash! When the irate mother asked the director what he was thinking, he answered that he was "trying to save the family money using a budget airline." Clearly, if you are considering a camp far from home, you need to work closely with the director to make sure that your camper is comfortable with the travel arrangement.

☼ **It's worth it** Even if you prefer your child attend a camp closer to home, there may be something about a specific program that makes the travel worth it. For example, if your child wants to specialize in sailing or mountain climbing, you'll need to choose a camp that meets those needs. One family deliberately chose a well-established fine arts camp for their theater-buff daughter even though it was at considerable distance from home. In this particular case, the father, a pediatrician, volunteered to act as camp doctor for two of the eight weeks his child was enrolled.

A parent may have a preference for a certain camp because she was a camper there herself, even if she no longer lives in the area. One mother who would have preferred a camp closer to home for her son, chose her own former camp which was more than 200 miles away. One of its advantages, the mother, believed was that the director, a former camper, was a childhood friend and she knew the camp would be well-run.

☆ **Diversity** While your camper may not see as many familiar faces in a camp far from home, this may be just what he (and you) wants. Often kids want to separate their camp life from the lives they lead the rest of the year. It's fun to have the opportunity to begin a program with a "clean slate." Sometimes youngsters feel "defined" and "limited" when they are in a program with many of the same kids who they see during the school year. This is an opportunity to meet kids who don't already have preconceived ideas about who your youngster is. One former camper recalls the "freedom" she felt when she went to camp where she didn't know a soul.

☆ **The distance doesn't bother the camper (or his parents)** For many youngsters, traveling alone, even by airplane, isn't scary, it's exciting. Many may have already done it. Assuming the camp has made appropriate travel arrangements, and depending on the maturity, sophistication, and sense of adventure of your child, you and she may be comfortable with a camp that is far from home.

Parents should figure out in advance what they will do if there is an emergency requiring them to get to camp quickly. For example, one camper attended a program six hours away from his home, but less than 45 minutes away from his grandparents. This gave his parents comfort— even though there was never an occasion to call for help.

When choosing a camp far from home, you and your camper need to discuss what that means in practical terms. Point out that once your camper arrives on site, the distance won't really be an issue. Mail generally takes the same amount of time to reach camp no matter where you live, so you can stay in close touch even if the miles separating you are far. But be honest if the distance means that only one (if any) parent will be able to attend visiting day.

Talk to the camp director before making a final decision to enroll your child in a program far from home to be sure that the program has handled this type of situation before. You probably don't want your child to be the only camper not from the area.

Size Matters

It's hard to know, especially if you've never seen an overnight camp program, if size makes a difference. Depending upon how well organized the program is, the answer is: maybe.

You don't want a camp so small that your child is limited in activities or friends. On the other hand, you don't want a program where your youngster is lost in the shuffle. The issue is not only numbers, but also how the camp breaks down the campers into manageable groups. If possible, there should be a minimum of two bunks for each age group so that your camper has a large enough group from which to choose friends. Too small a camp—fewer than 100 campers—can mean if a clique forms your child may be left out (especially if the other campers already know each other or met at camp the previous year). On the other hand, a small camp may seem less intimidating to a first-time camper.

However, if the program is too large, it's difficult for the campers to know other kids outside their age group. It's also harder for the camp to offer all-inclusive activities. One of the fondest memories of many former campers is the contact between the age groups—the senior campers adopting the younger ones—and the sense of closeness that develops among the campers. There's something very nice about walking across the lawn greeting by name everyone who passes. It's also fun when counselors assigned to a different age group know all the campers by name because the program is small enough to encourage that kind of interaction. Furthermore, programs that would include all campers, like campfires and cookouts, become unwieldy and difficult to organize if the program is too large. One large camp used to schedule two bonfires in a night to accommodate all its campers. It's difficult (but not impossible) to build a sense of camp unity and spirit under those circumstances.

Single-Sex or Coed

A strong case can be made for choosing a single-gender camp, but an equally strong one can be made for coed camps. You know your child and your own philosophy about single-sex versus coed programs. One former camper, however, remembers his own disgruntlement over attending both an all-boys school *and* an all-boys camp. Even though he individually loved both institutions, he believed that a single-gender environment, year-round, was limiting.

ADVANTAGES OF A SINGLE-SEX CAMP
- ☼ Social (boy-girl) issues are kept to a minimum, especially for older campers. Eliminating the distraction of "how you look" in front of

the opposite sex (both literally and figuratively) helps put the focus back on the primary goals of a good camp experience: developing skills, making new friends, taking risks.

☼ Most campers attend coed schools so a single-sex camp can be an enriching and different environment.

☼ There is a depth to the friendships that are developed without the distraction of or the competition for the affections of the opposite sex.

☼ The intensity of play and skill development is enhanced when the camper isn't worried or distracted by social issues.

ADVANTAGES OF A COED CAMP

☼ If you have children of the opposite sex, it can be easier if you can find one camp that suits them both. Many parents say that while they might in theory prefer a single-sex camp, the mechanics of getting both kids off to two different programs and the corresponding effort of visiting two different camps on visiting day, wasn't worth it.

☼ Some parents believe that coed camps are less competitive than single-sex camps. The theory is that because there is a more social atmosphere in the camp, the intensity of play is reduced. For those families looking for a less competitive program, that's an advantage.

General Interest or Specialty Camp

General interest camps offer diverse programming with dozens of activities and sports for the campers. *A special interest camp* focuses primarily on a specific sport (e.g., basketball, baseball, football, soccer, etc.) or activity (e.g., dramatics, music, computers).

As a rule of thumb, most experts advise sending first-time campers to a general interest camp. It gives kids an opportunity to try a wide range of activities and interests before settling on any one area. Furthermore, most general interest camps have more staff training and greater sensitivity to the emotional demands of a first-time camper. At specialty camps, there aren't as many "warm fuzzies." The emphasis is on the sport/hobby/interest. If the camper is engaged, terrific. If not, if there are adjustment problems, there may not be much help available. Most of the counselors are hired for their expertise in the specialty, not for their attention to childhood development. (See chapter 6 for more information on specialty camps.)

A good program at a general interest camp will satisfy and challenge the interests and activities of all the campers. Even if you suspect that your athletically or artistically talented youngster will surpass the level of competition he will find at camp, you may decide that you prefer to send him to a program that tests and encourages him in other areas. Perhaps you don't want him to focus on baseball all summer, but would rather he improve his swimming or try out for the camp play.

On the other hand, especially for an older first-time camper, there are some kids who are very focused on a specific sport or activity (e.g., computers, music) and want to spend the summer pursuing that interest. One ten-year-old Little Leaguer was in baseball heaven when he went to a specialty camp and spent an entire week devoted to playing baseball, talking baseball, watching baseball videos, etc. Most specialty camps hold a series of one week sessions, with campers generally enrolled for only one or two weeks per season.

Specialty camps are best for the child who is *personally* committed to the sport or activity. Don't send your child to this type of camp because you think he should improve his skills. Playing any sport (or computers or musical instrument) for 10 to 12 hours a day—unless you love the activity—will kill any burgeoning interest faster than the speed of lightning. Specialty camps are for campers who want to immerse themselves in the subject, surrounded by like-minded campers.

Session Length: Full Summer or Less

When looking at camps, you want to know how long most of the children stay. You may prefer, or have no objection, to a full summer program, which lasts seven or eight weeks. Or for family or budget considerations, you may prefer a shorter program. Some camps run sessions of varying lengths, from a minimum of one week to a range of combinations (two, three, four, five, or six weeks).

Some camps offer a full-summer program only. There are several advantages:

✳ All campers come and go at the same time. It can be a problem if your child has made a good friend at camp, who leaves after two weeks, while your youngster is staying for another six weeks. Furthermore, all the campers are going through the emotional adjustment to camp at the same time.

☼ All campers get the same program. It can be disappointing if your child is staying for the first month of camp, and color war (an intra-camp competition), often the highlight of the experience, isn't held until the second half of the summer.

☼ The campers have time to build relationships and to sample the wide variety of activities offered.

☼ A full summer program meets your family needs.

But many families prefer a shorter camp experience for their child. They may decide that their child isn't ready for a longer program; they want time for a family vacation; their budget doesn't permit a full-summer program.

Also there seems to be a different philosophy about camp session lengths on the two coasts. In the traditional camps in the East, it's not unusual to find only full-summer programs. On the West Coast, however, most campers attend for shorter periods, generally two-week sessions. Although campers can elect to stay for longer, usually not longer than a month, they're actually bridging two, two-week sessions. As the director of one camp in California described his market, "In any two weeks, we would expect to have 200 campers staying for two weeks, 40 staying for four weeks, and one or two staying longer."

In the East, a new camping trend seems to be developing to meet the needs of families who want a full camp program in a shorter time. Several directors now offer the full camp program, from opening day to color war, but in a four-week session. Each summer the camp offers two, four-week programs and campers can enroll for either session (no one other than the staff stays the entire summer).

AFFILIATED WITH A RELIGIOUS MOVEMENT OR SECULAR?

You may decide to limit your camp search to programs affiliated with your family's religion. These types of camps generally incorporate a religious component into the program, while still offering regular camping activities.

Be sure to ask how the camp includes the religious component into their daily or weekly program. Remember that some camps limit the religious component to holidays, while still others include daily prayers as part of the camp day, and may celebrate only holidays particular to that religion. For example, you may want to ask if the camp will celebrate Independence Day (July 4). Although this is a national holiday, some more religiously observant camps may choose to de-emphasize its celebration.

You also want to check the qualifications of the counselors. Some camps may consider religious observance more important than educational training or experience.

Advantages

☼ Children become more familiar and comfortable with the traditions and customs of their religious heritage.

☼ If your family is religiously observant, having your child in an affiliated camp reinforces what is being taught at home and facilitates observance of holidays and customs.

☼ If your family is not observant, having your child in this type of camp often helps to build a place for religion in the family structure. Many parents believe that having a child in a church/synagogue camp forced them to focus on religious issues they had ignored and gave them a welcoming community in which to sort out these issues.

☼ The child finds a peer group within his religion, which can reinforce his commitment to the faith.

Disadvantages

The main disadvantages of a church/synagogue camp are:

☼ Lack of diversity. Most, if not all the campers, will share the same religious background, which means that your child may not be exposed to a variety of customs, traditions, language, experiences.

☼ Conflicting value systems. If your family is either less or more religiously observant than the camp, your child may find the contrast between home and camp difficult to understand. Much depends on both your own and the camp's attitude and how each of you deals with the differences.

Some programs are comfortable and used to dealing with the issue, others may be more judgmental or even evangelical.

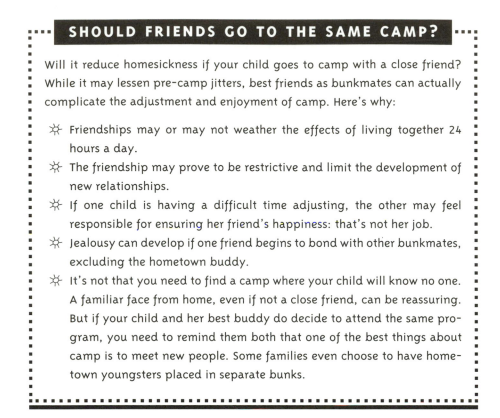

SHOULD FRIENDS GO TO THE SAME CAMP?

Will it reduce homesickness if your child goes to camp with a close friend? While it may lessen pre-camp jitters, best friends as bunkmates can actually complicate the adjustment and enjoyment of camp. Here's why:

☼ Friendships may or may not weather the effects of living together 24 hours a day.

☼ The friendship may prove to be restrictive and limit the development of new relationships.

☼ If one child is having a difficult time adjusting, the other may feel responsible for ensuring her friend's happiness: that's not her job.

☼ Jealousy can develop if one friend begins to bond with other bunkmates, excluding the hometown buddy.

☼ It's not that you need to find a camp where your child will know no one. A familiar face from home, even if not a close friend, can be reassuring. But if your child and her best buddy do decide to attend the same program, you need to remind them both that one of the best things about camp is to meet new people. Some families even choose to have hometown youngsters placed in separate bunks.

BUDGET NEEDS

There are good sleepaway camp programs that meet every family's budget. According to the American Camping Association, resident camps range from $15 to $120 per day. On average, private sleepaway camps charge between $1,800 and $3,500 for four-week sessions. A full-summer program will range from $3,500 to $6,000. Nonprofit camps will cost between $1,100 and $2,700 for a four-week session, and $2,500 to $4,000 for eight weeks. Two-week programs generally run between $650 and $1,600.

Many camps, especially those sponsored by nonprofit organizations, offer some financial assistance to families in need. Don't let a limited family budget eliminate summer camp for your child. The American Camping Association reports that 85 percent of camps surveyed reported offering some level of financial assistance.

Some families have also been able to "trade services" in exchange for a lower camp fee. One mother served as the camp nurse in exchange for her son's camp tuition. Other than when he was stung by a bee, he saw very little of his mother that summer!

Another mother worked as a camp's on-site office manager. A schoolteacher with summers off, she made a deal with the camp director. She would manage the business operations of the camp during the summer, and in exchange, in addition to her son attending camp free, she received a house at the camp and a baby-sitter for her younger children (who enjoyed the camp's facilities as well).

Another family traded landscaping work (the family business) for a discount on camp fees. The point is: ask.

Camp Uniform?

Some camps have a strict uniform policy. Campers must wear, on-site and off-site, regulation T-shirts and shorts (bought through a camp outfitter). The underlying philosophy is that uniforms reduce wardrobe competition among campers and create a sense of camp unity.

Other camps permit the children to wear their own clothes while on-site, but insist that the kids wear a camp T-shirt and shorts when off-site. Besides building unity, it also makes it easier to keep track of members of the group.

Still others have regulation uniforms (swimsuits) for inter-camp competition. And some camp programs have no uniform policy at all.

And even those camps that have strict uniform codes, generally permit certain days when the campers can wear what they want.

You need to decide if a uniform policy is an important issue to you or your child. For one mother of a preteen who thought her daughter was already too clothes crazy, she welcomed a uniform camp so *the emphasis shifted from what her daughter wore to what she did.*

Keep in mind that it does add to the cost of the summer to outfit your child with uniforms for camp (since you probably will still have to purchase a summer wardrobe.)

WHO MAKES THE DECISION?

Choosing a summer camp can be a wonderful experience that you can share with your child. In fact, it's important that she feels that her opinion is taken seriously as you look at various programs. Furthermore, without her cooperation and enthusiasm, your child may not develop the proper attitude and may not fully enjoy camp, no matter how good the program may be.

That said, adults bring experience and perspective to the process. It's easy for an eight-year-old to get dazzled by the camp video or be impressed by the computer games on-site, and miss important health and safety issues. That's where the grown-ups have to step in and point out "what's wrong with this picture."

Finally, as adults have learned about decision making in the workplace, if you make someone feel like he is part of the process, he becomes "vested" in the outcome. If your child believes that he is part of the family decision about when and where he will go to camp, he is more committed to making it succeed.

In the next chapter, we'll discuss the nitty-gritty of finding the perfect sleepaway camp for your child.

Chapter **3**

FINDING THE RIGHT SLEEPAWAY CAMP:
THE SEARCH CAN BE FUN

I remember the camp director lugging in this big carousel of slides. My dad set up our home movie screen in the living room and we sat on the sofa watching. With the click of each slide, the camp became more and more real to me. I pictured myself on the waterfront, in the arts and crafts building, around the campfire. Years later, when we started looking for a summer camp for our son, the director made an appointment to visit our home. I made my husband bring up from the basement that same old home movie screen, but, of course, I'd forgotten that nobody watches slides anymore. The director brought a camp video!

Once you've made the decision to send your child to sleepaway camp, finding and choosing the right program is the next step. But which one is right for *your child* out of the more than 5,500 overnight camps in the United States? How do you make this important decision?

WHEN TO START YOUR SEARCH

Ideally, you would begin searching for a camp a full year before you plan to enroll your child. Why? Because that will give you an opportunity to visit summer camps while they are in session. The marketing materials you receive will undoubtedly put a glossy shine on the camps they are promoting, but an on-site visit puts things in perspective. Not only does it permit you the opportunity to actually see what they mean when they refer to the camp as a "rustic retreat," but it also gives you an opportunity to observe the campers. *Do these campers look and behave like your child?* You begin to get a feel for these kinds of places: where they put their emphasis, the intensity of the program, the "personality" of the camp and its staff.

Furthermore, even if you decide that this particular camp is not right for your child, it gives you a frame of reference. As one mother pointed out: "It wasn't until I saw a camp with almost 300 campers, and then compared it to another one we visited, which had only 125 campers, did I fully understand the issue of camp size and its impact on a program." Especially if a parent has never attended sleepaway camp as a child, it's helpful to visit an overnight camp just to get a general idea of how these programs work.

If you can't begin your search the summer before, it's best to start by late fall. Good camps fill up quickly (and many give a discount for those campers who enroll by December 31). To give your family as much choice as possible, start your search early.

HOW TO START

Even if you think you have already decided on a specific camp, you would be wise to keep an open mind and look at several programs before making a commitment. This will give you a point of comparison. Here are some ways to find camp programs:

☼ Of course, word of mouth is generally the best resource. Other families in your community may recommend or criticize a certain camp. Consider the source and listen carefully to the criticisms. The problems reported may not be an issue for you or may reflect different child-rearing practices or expectations.

☼ Check your *church or synagogue.* Many religious institutions sponsor summer programs.

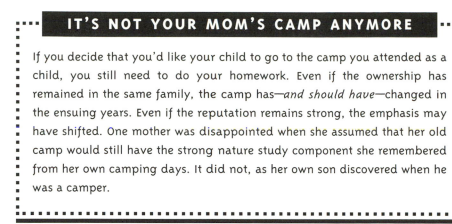

IT'S NOT YOUR MOM'S CAMP ANYMORE

If you decide that you'd like your child to go to the camp you attended as a child, you still need to do your homework. Even if the ownership has remained in the same family, the camp has—*and should have*—changed in the ensuing years. Even if the reputation remains strong, the emphasis may have shifted. One mother was disappointed when she assumed that her old camp would still have the strong nature study component she remembered from her own camping days. It did not, as her own son discovered when he was a camper.

- ✷ Your *pediatrician* is another good resource.
- ✷ Check your *library* for camp guides. *Peterson's* publishes a yearly compendium of summer camps and teen tours. (See Appendix 4 for resources.)
- ✷ *Newspapers, magazines, and specialty magazines* (sport, computer, etc.) often carry advertisements about summer programs.
- ✷ Go *on-line.* Many summer camps now maintain web sites. Also check with parenting forums. Many parents post queries about camps on electronic bulletin boards. It's one way to get a reference for a camp, but don't use it as a substitute for a phone call if you are seriously checking references.
- ✷ Visit a *camp fair.* A smorgasbord of summer camp possibilities in one place, this is an opportunity to visit dozens of booths and get a quick overview of a variety of programs. Usually held midwinter in many large cities, these fairs are normally very crowded so you'll probably have only time for brief chats with camp directors (or their representatives), but you can arrange appointments to meet at a later time for a more thorough discussion.

Private Camp Adviser

Some families use a private camp adviser to help them narrow down the choices. Generally camp advisers don't charge parents, but instead collect a 10 to 15 percent commission from camps for each youngster who enrolls after referral. Some private camp advisers prefer to charge a flat fee ($400 or more) to parents in order to avoid the appearance of a conflict of interest. But frankly, there is no guarantee either way, so parents must still do their homework. Check the camp adviser's references: Ask for the names of families who have used the service. Call and ask what they liked and didn't like about the adviser—and how best to use the service. You might also want to check any camp advisory service with your Better Business Bureau. After interviewing you and your child, either in person or over the phone, a camp adviser will recommend several programs. An important advantage of using a camp adviser is that an experienced professional has visited most, if not all, of the camps she is recommending. She keeps abreast of changes in ownership or management (which should prompt another on-site visit), and is able to compare and contrast hundreds of programs.

While the adviser can help to refine the options, and perhaps recommend some camps a family might not have otherwise considered, parents must still personally interview camp directors and check camp references.

You can find a camp adviser via word of mouth (probably the best method) or through the yellow pages.

Lights, Camera, Video

Once you've narrowed your search to four or five possibilities, call the camp (or e-mail via the web site) and ask for additional information. In addition to a brochure and/or printed literature, most private camps now have a promotional video. While a video will give you a visual image of the camp, parents—and kids—need to understand that these videos are marketing tools, designed to present the program in the best light. Think of them as infomercials.

Watch the video with your child, but let her take the lead in discussing it. After watching a few you'll learn what she thinks is important in a camp—and what she can live without. One mother was surprised when her daughter checked each video for scenes of a ropes course. She was about to eliminate one camp possibility (which otherwise seemed a good match), until the director explained that a new ropes course had been added since the video was produced.

While it's understandable that your youngster may become excited or totally turned off by something she sees in the video, it's important to help her see the "big picture." The whole camp selection process is instructive on several levels:

Your child learns about "truth in advertising." She needs to understand that camp videos can be similar to the television ads for toys: The reality doesn't always match up to the image on the screen.

Your child learns about compromise in choice. Choosing a camp may require a number of trade-offs. The size, location, and other activities may be perfect, but the tennis program is only adequate. Okay, perhaps that means that your camper's tennis skills won't improve much over the summer. Can she take lessons during the school year? Working through this process, your child will have an opportunity to learn how to choose what's important to her and what she's willing to trade off. Listen carefully to what your youngster is saying: It will help you decide what you, the parent, are willing to compromise in making this decision.

The Camp Video

Although it's primarily a marketing tool, you'll want to watch the video closely for clues about the camp's philosophy and strengths. As David Betz, vice president of Camp TV, which produces videos for camps and schools explains: "Videos are a neat way to do long distance travel in your living room, but they should never be a replacement for personal visits either to the camp or with the camp representatives." Here's what to look for in a camp video:

1. **How old is the video?**

   If there is no date on it, then you "guesstimate" based on the kids' clothing, hair length, and background music. Your child may be turned off if the camp video looks too old—thinking that kids and music seem out-of-date.

   No matter how new the video is, you'll want to ask the director what's new in the program since the video was produced (both in terms of activities and in physical changes to the camp). A good camp is constantly updating and introducing new programs—and the maintenance/upkeep of the camp also requires yearly update.

2. **Does the video answer your questions about the camp?**

   Clearly you will have additional issues to raise with the director, but the video should give a comprehensive overview of the program, daily activities, and camp highlights.

3. What does the video emphasize?

If you're looking for a camp that stresses sports, and 5 minutes of the 10-minute video is on the many talent shows the campers produce each year, you may be looking at the wrong program.

4. Do the kids look like they're having fun?

Again, the video is a promotional tool, but what were the kids doing—and would your own child enjoy these activities.

5. What level of sports were shown in the video?

Did the sports program highlighted in the video look too advanced for your child or did it appear that there were different levels of play? Unless you are choosing a specialty camp, there should be a wide range of proficiency levels in camp sports—a place for everyone, as well as the potential to move into a more competitive group as your child improves.

6. What did the video stress?

The camp literature should have explained the underlying philosophy of the camp: Did the video complement the printed word? You may also have to consider to whom the video is directed. Some camps deliberately choose to direct the message to the future camper, with little specific information for the parents (for example, counselor-camper ratio). But the accompanying printed literature should present the information that a parent will need. Similarly, if a video is solely directed at the parents, you may wonder, "where's the fun?"

7. What was your and your child's general impression after watching the video?

One mother, who couldn't quite put her finger on what bothered her about a certain camp video, could only agree when her prospective camper commented: "It's not me." That comment prompted a conversation between mother and child. They concluded that the camp seemed "too intense."

ON-SITE VISITS

If you have the opportunity to visit summer camps while they are in session, do so. You'll learn the most by direct observation and conversation. Call for an appointment at least a week in advance. It's possible that the director may ask you to choose another day for a visit if many of the campers will be off-site (for an overnight campout, an inter-camp sports activity, a trip), if it's parents' weekend, or if it's between sessions (if it's not a full-summer program). The camp will mail (or fax) you directions, and include promotional brochures and the video. If you can, review the material before you go to camp. It will probably answer many of the basic questions about the program, but it will also give you the chance to compare the media image of the camp to reality.

Leave yourself at least two hours (preferably three) to spend at the camp. It's tempting to try and see as many camps in the area as possible, but you will need time to tour, observe, and chat. You want to be able to observe several activities for the entire period. This will give you a chance to see how the counselors juggle the demands of campers (those at different skill levels, those with different attention spans). You'll also see how they handle transitions from one activity to another. And it will give you an opportunity to observe directly the safety precautions they take to ensure an accident-free program.

An on-site visit is not only a chance to see the setting and facilities, but also the opportunity to observe firsthand the administration and staff in action. While not all of the counselors you observe may return the following year when your child enrolls, the type of counselors hired, the method of staff supervision by the director, the tone, attitude, and expectations of the camp community do continue as long as the owners/directors remain the same.

If your child is with you on the tour, you'll want to see how much of the visit has been geared to capture *her* interest. Does the tour guide include the youngster in the conversation? Does the guide listen and *respectfully* answer your child's questions? Does the guide linger while your child explores an interesting activity or facility? *How the guide interacts with your youngster reveals the camp's attitude and relationship to kids.*

Here's what to look for (see Appendix 2 for a checklist):

THE DIRECTOR

The camp director may or may not be your tour guide, but if not, be sure and meet her before leaving. The director sets the tone for the camp. You want to know if this is someone you can trust to take care of your child for the summer.

Is she a *hands-on* administrator: walking about the camp, talking directly with campers and counselors, offering encouragement, supervision, accessibility? Does she know the names of all the campers she meets? Most camps prefer to schedule visits after the program has been in session for a few weeks. By then, a good director should know the members of her camp community by name. Or does she spend most of the day in the office doing paperwork? Where is her camp residence?

THE COUNSELORS

The counselors are the core of any camp program. If they aren't mature, attentive, kind, caring, sensitive, imaginative, empathetic, and skilled, then it doesn't matter how great are the facilities and activities. You want your child to be safe and have fun and *the counselors are directly responsible for both*. So pay special attention to how the counselors interact with the campers.

* **Are the counselors involved with the campers—or with each other?** During an activity, are they supervising and interacting with the kids—or chatting among themselves?
* **During a game or activity, is praise freely given to all campers—or just to the superstars?**   And what kind of praise is given? Is it specific (the best kind), such as during a soccer game: "That was a great throw-in. You kept both feet on the ground and threw it right down the line to one of your teammates." That's more effective than just "good job."
* **Are the specialty counselors (sports, waterfront, arts and crafts, drama, etc.) good teachers?**   It's great to have college varsity tennis players as the camp tennis coaches or professional actors to direct the camp musicals, but can they actually teach the skills and work with kids? Some people are good at what they do, but can't translate that enthusiasm or skill to kids. Don't get dazzled by flashy credentials. When you observe an activity, do the drills make educational sense and are they fun (after all, this is supposed to be fun)?

PHYSICAL LAYOUT

As you tour the camp, pay close attention to the facilities. Are the buildings well maintained and recently painted or are they peeling, showing clear signs of a lack of maintenance? You're not looking for dozens of new buildings. There may, in fact, be a well-worn or rustic quality to the buildings, but that's different from being neglected.

☼ Bunks

Are they buildings or tents?

How many beds are in each bunk?

Are they individual cots or bunk beds?

Does the camper get to choose which bed she wants? (Suppose she doesn't want a top bunk?)

Where do the campers store their gear?

How crowded are the bunks? Does it appear that they have over-booked and the campers are cramped into a too small space?

How clean are the bunks? While you're not looking for any to pass the white-glove test, the beds should be made (by the campers), the clothing should be in individual cubbies.

Where do the counselors sleep? There should be at least one counselor sleeping in each bunk.

☼ Bathrooms

This is a *big* issue for many campers (and their parents).

Where are the toilets? Does each bunk have its own toilets or do the children have to walk to a common bathhouse? For younger children, especially, it can be a problem if they have to leave their bunks to use the toilet. If so, does the child go to the toilet by herself at night? Is the path lighted?

Are there showers in each bunk? (Sometimes there are toilet facilities in each bunk, but a common shower house.)

Many campers are concerned about privacy—are there individual shower stalls?

Do campers have to walk in their bathrobes/pajamas to the showers?

If it's a coed camp; how separate are the shower facilities?

Who cleans the facilities—and how often?

☼ Swimming pool/waterfront

Is the pool large enough so the campers swim easily without bumping into each other?

Are there clearly marked, separate waterfront areas for swimming, boating, water skiing, diving?

Is there boating, sailing, and water skiing equipment? What's the level of supervision? Is there a counselor in the power boat when a camper is water skiing? Do the campers always wear life jackets when engaged in these water sports?

☼ The grounds

Are the playing fields freshly reseeded and mowed?

Are the trails clearly marked?

Is the equipment in excellent condition?

☼ Dining hall

Is there enough seating space for the whole camp to eat in one session?

Must bunks eat together?

Can campers eat with friends in different age groups?

Is it buffet style or are the campers served? If served, by whom?

What if the camper doesn't like the main selection? Are peanut butter and jelly always available? Is there a salad bar?

Are menus posted so campers can see lunch/dinner selections?

Are snacks served? Is there a canteen?

What's for breakfast, lunch, and dinner on that day?

Who is the kitchen director? How long has he been on staff? What are his credentials?

What are the safety and cleanliness standards for the kitchen and staff? Is it inspected by local authorities?

☼ Arts and crafts

Is there sufficient seating for every camper?

What are the craft projects? How much emphasis is placed on process (learning the skill), and how much emphasis is on the end result?

Are there enough supplies and tools so that many campers can participate in a crafts project? For example, is there more than one pottery wheel?

Are the crafts projects cookie-cutter duplicates of each other or is creativity and imagination stressed? For example, for ceramics, are the campers merely painting manufactured objects or do they take the clay, mold it into the shape they want, and design the piece from start to finish? Is it a precut birdhouse that the camper merely glues together and paints, or does the camper learn to use a saw and cut the wood pieces herself?

SAFETY

You want your child to have fun, of course, but safety should be interwoven into the very fabric of the camp program and facilities. Safety measures should dictate how the activities are run, as well as the physical layout of the camp. As you tour the camp, take note:

☀ Are there smoke alarms in every bunk and every camp building? Does the camp hold a fire drill at least once per session? Where is the fire department? At what distance?

☀ Is there a list of safety regulations clearly posted for each activity? Do the counselors review with the campers the regulations before the activity begins?

☀ Do the campers and counselors wear protective equipment (athletic cup, shin guards, mouth guards, etc.) for sports? Counselors need to serve as role models on safety issues. Kids need to see that it's "cool" to wear safety gear.

☀ Are there warm-up and cooldown exercises before each sports activity (proper conditioning is essential for reducing injuries)?

☀ Is there a higher counselor-camper ratio in potentially dangerous situations: ropes courses, waterfront, riflery, gymnastics, archery, woodworking?

☀ Do the campers and counselors wear protective equipment when using woodworking tools? Do they wear protective goggles? It's not enough that the protective equipment is available: Do the counselors insist that it is worn and in fact wear it themselves when working.

☀ On the waterfront: Does the lifeguard insist on the buddy system and call frequent buddy checks during swim? Is there a controlled but fun atmosphere during free swim? Is the diving board activity closely monitored (and the area in front of the board kept clear)? Do all water skiers wear life vests? What kind of swim tests are given before and during the season to monitor progress? Is there a written checklist that a camper must sign when she leaves the waterfront (in order to be sure who is and who isn't in the water)?

- On the playing fields: Are the fields at a distance from the normal camp traffic? If a ballplayer hits a home run, where will it land? Where is the archery field and/or riflery range located? Must all archers put down their bows before retrieving the arrows?
- On the ropes courses: How many harnesses are used to secure the climber? How many counselors hold the lines?
- For gymnasts: Are there spotters at all activities? Are there protective mats? Are campers evaluated for skill level before beginning any activity?
- For horseback riders: Who is in charge of the riding instruction? Who is responsible for the daily care of the horses? Do the horses look healthy? Are the barns clean and the individual stalls mucked out? Are the saddles, cinches, halters and bits well maintained? Are the trails frequently monitored for safety? Are the riding rings free of debris? Do all riders, beginners and expert, wear protective hats when astride a horse? Are the riding trails and rings far enough from a road or riflery range that a horse won't be easily spooked?

After the Tour

After the tour, be sure and leave time in your schedule to talk and ask questions. But you will probably have additional questions later, after you've had time to think about what you saw. A good camp will follow up with a phone call in about a week to ask if you—or your child—have additional questions.

HOUSE CALLS

You may not have the opportunity for any on-site visits, but in some sense, the camp can come to you. If possible, the camp director, or representative, will visit your home to discuss the program and your concerns.

GROUP MEETING OR ONE-ON-ONE

Ideally, the meeting with the camp director is solely with your family. It's a chance for you and your child to get to know the person who will be responsible for your child's safety and good time. One mother, worried that she wouldn't know *how* to recognize a good camp program, was reassured by her own mother's advice: "You'll find a director whom you trust to take care of your child. The rest will follow."

That's one of the reasons you want the time and privacy to interview the director. You want to see how he interacts with your child. You want to see what he stresses in his presentation. And you want the liberty and freedom from embarrassment to ask any and all the questions you or your child may have—no matter how small or insignificant they may seem.

Sometimes a director will ask if he can combine the home visit with another family or two. Say no if at all possible, although it may be difficult given the director's schedule and logistics. If you must combine the visit with another family, insist that each family have a few moments *alone* with the director for personal issues.

SHOULD SIBLINGS BE INCLUDED?

Again the purpose of the house call is to permit you and your potential camper to get to know the director and learn about the program. If younger (or older) siblings are willing to sit and listen quietly—sure, include them with the thought that this might, at a later point, be a good program for them too. But if not, if the little one is likely to have difficulty controlling herself or might distract from the presentation, make other arrangements. The home visit generally lasts about an hour and a half. It may be your only chance to meet face-to-face before camp starts—use the time wisely.

What's on the Agenda: The Nitty-Gritty

After a brief presentation about the camp (assuming you've already seen the camp video), the director will ask if you have any questions. Now is the time to get specifics about the camp and how your child will fit into the program. You are looking for a director who can answer your questions clearly and in some detail. For example, if he hedges and says: "There are so many activities or programs, I can't even list them all," that may be an indication that he's not a "hands-on" director. You want someone who really knows the camp, the program, the nitty-gritty about his community. Here are some areas that you'll want to cover.

1. **Beyond numbers**

While the director should tell you the staff-camper ratio, you want to know what these numbers actually mean in day-to-day camp life.

- What is the counselor-camper ratio? The American Camping Association recommends:

Age	Counselor to Camper Ratio
6 to 8 years old	1 staff for every 6 campers
9 to 14 years old	1 staff for every 8 campers
15 to 18 years old	1 staff for every 10 campers

- How many campers and counselors are in each bunk?
- What is the instructor-camper ratio for skills classes such as swimming, tennis, riding?
- Do additional counselors accompany campers on off-site trips?

2. **Who's in charge**

Ask who runs the camp on a daily basis. You want to know the background and credentials for the camp director. Is the director also the owner? If not, who owns the camp and is he located on-site? That's not necessary, but again you want to get the feel of the program and who's in charge.

You also want to know the longevity of the director, owner, and staff. It's not unusual for camps to have remained in the same family for decades. Be wary of a camp that is "breaking in" a new on-site director. You want to know the background and experience of the new personnel. Often it is someone who has been on staff for many years, but check.

You also want to know if the camp is accredited by the American Camping Association (ACA), a national organization that establishes uniform standards for reviewing camps on a continual basis. Accreditation is a voluntary process by which camps are evaluated every three years on nearly 300 standards affecting health and safety, camp management, personnel, programming, and facilities. However, not all camps choose to undergo the lengthy accreditation process. And even if a camp has been accredited by the ACA, you still need to make sure it's the right program for your child, as well as do the usual reference check.

3. The counseling staff

Since counselors can make or break a program, how the director staffs his program is critical.

☼ Where does he recruit his counselors? Many camps recruit counselors on college campuses. Others also recruit overseas for counselors because there's a strong market of young people interested in coming to America for the summer (most tack on a few weeks to tour after the camp season). This can add to the cultural diversity of a camp, but it can also change the dynamics (for good or bad) of the camp because of the cultural differences.

☼ How is the camp counseling staff organized? Who supervises the bunk counselors? Are regular meetings of camp staff held? What is discussed at these meetings? To whom can a counselor turn if he is having difficulty with a camper?

☼ What are the credentials of the specialty counselors? Do they have any other responsibilities in the camp?

☼ How many counselors are former campers? That's a strong comment on the strength of the program when young adults choose to return to a beloved camp as a counselor.

☼ How many counselors are returning from the previous season? Again, it's a positive comment on the camp if many counselors choose to return for a second (or more) season. Of course, most young adults eventually "age out" of the camp counselor job. It's a good sign if more than 35 percent of the staff are returning from the previous season. Often the percentage is even higher at better camps.

☼ How many under-18-year-old counselors will be supervising my camper? Junior counselor/counselor-in-training (CIT) positions are common at many camps. These jobs are frequently sought as the answer for the mid-teen adolescent, but this is not the kind of direct supervision you expect from a quality program. (See chapter 7 for a discussion of CIT programs for teenagers.) Junior counselors should be assistants, always under the direct supervision of a more mature counselor. *They should not be counted as part of the staff-camper ratio.*

☼ What kind of background check do you run on your counselors and staff? Physical, emotional, or sexual abuse by counselors is extremely rare, but it is every parent's nightmare.

The difficulty is that there is no national, computerized system that a camp can tap to check its counselors. At a minimum, camps should be conducting their own intensive reference checks. You also want to know what the camp does to protect the children from potentially dangerous situations: For example, many camps require that no counselor is ever completely alone with a camper.

☼ What kind of training program does the camp require of its counselors? Every camp should have a pre-camp counselor training program. Ask about it. It should be more than just songs and games. Make sure the camp is training their counselors for coping with serious problems like homesickness and bunk tensions.

4. The facilities

Inquire about any new construction being done at camp during the off-season, as well as regular maintenance. What is the camp acreage? It should be at least 50 acres, with 25 to 40 acres for the actual campsite. The additional acreage provides privacy and beauty. But also check into:

☼ the camp's water supply
☼ sewage and refuse disposal
☼ mosquito, flies, and tick control.

This isn't idle curiosity. These are basic health and safety issues.

☼ Is laundry done on-site? Most camps send laundry out once a week, but many also do towels on-site because of the constant use.

5. Medical issues

In addition to discussing any special medical needs of your child, you want to know about the medical care your child will find at camp (see chapter 5 on medical care at camp). Most camps are comfortable dispensing routine medications, including Ritalin and allergy injections. Camps generally have established relationships with local dentists and orthodontists to handle routine and emergency dental visits. You also want to know:

☼ the credentials of the camp medical staff. Is the doctor a pediatrician or general/family practitioner? While some camps rely on a rotating medical staff drawn from the parents of the campers, this could be a problem. Sometimes specialists, such as dermatologists or surgeons, assume the responsibility of acting as camp doctor, but may not be as familiar with common childhood ailments. What are the credentials of the nursing staff? How long have the doctor and nursing staff been affiliated with the camp? One camp had established a relationship with the family practitioner program at a nearby medical facility. Each summer a senior resident served as the camp's on-site doctor. There were several experienced nurses, and the camp medical staff was under the supervision of the medical facility's senior doctors.

☀ Of the medical staff, who is actually on-site? What are the hours when children are seen? Who stays with a child who is in the infirmary?

☀ Describe the camp infirmary? Who is admitted to the infirmary and how long can a camper stay in the infirmary?

☀ Are parents notified if the child is ill or only if the child is admitted to the infirmary or taken to the local hospital?

☀ Where is the closest medical facility? How would a camper be transported there? If it is a small facility with limited services, what arrangements are there for access to more extensive and sophisticated medical care?

☀ How does the camp treat contagious diseases (these can be as mild as a cold, conjunctivitis, or head lice)?

☀ Do the camp fees include medical insurance? How does the camp handle health insurance if the child needs to be taken to the hospital? *Check with your own insurance carrier to determine your coverage.*

6. The camp program

Now is the time to review the camp's daily schedule. (See the following sample day at an overnight camp.)

☀ What times are reveille and taps?

☀ When are the meals and snacks (including canteen)?

☀ What is the rainy day program? What if it rains for several days in a row?

☀ Does the camp conduct religious services? Is attendance compulsory?

☀ Have the director rate the competition factor at the camp on a scale of 1 to 10? Where does *your* child feel comfortable? Are

A TYPICAL DAY AT CAMP

7:00 A.M.	Rise and shine. Prebreakfast activities like aerobics, early morning swim.
7:30	Flag raising and morning announcements
7:45	Breakfast
8:30	Cabin cleanup
9:00—10:15	First activity, may be skills, sports, crafts, hobbies, or instructional swim
10:20—11:15	Second activity, may be skills, sports, crafts, hobbies or instructional swim
11:25—11:55	Free swim
12:00	Lunch
12:30—1:30	Free time/rest period. Campers in bunks reading, writing, playing quiet games
1:45—3:00	Third activity, may be skills, sports, crafts, hobbies, or instructional swim
3:15—4:15	Fourth activity, may be skills, sports, crafts, hobbies, or instructional swim
4:25—4:55	Free swim
5:00—6:00	Free time. Campers can play pickup games, write, read, chat
6:00	Supper
7:30	Evening program for all campers
9:00	Lights out for younger campers
9:30	Lights out for older campers

there plenty of noncompetitive sports played? Again, you know your child, but even for the child who thrives on competition, you want an atmosphere where the emphasis isn't always on winning.

☼ Are there inter-camp teams? How are the members of the teams chosen?

☼ Are there special weekly or session events such as campfires, cookouts, sleepouts, or trips?

☀ Describe color war. There are lots of ways to handle this traditional end-of-season event. Some camps prefer to divide the campers into two teams, but this may increase the competitive nature of the event (someone wins, someone loses). If the camp divides the campers into four or more teams, the stress is more on fun and less on winning.

☀ Is there "downtime" built into the schedule?

☀ What kinds of crafts projects do campers have the opportunity to work on?

7. Camp adjustment

Especially for the first-time camper, you want to know how the camp staff helps ease the adjustment to camp. How does the director handle loneliness and homesickness? Ask if any child ever failed to adjust to camp. (The answer should be yes if it's an experienced director. Although rare, there are children who don't adjust and do leave the program. Usually, the camp and parents can't work together to resolve the issues. (See chapter 4 on homesickness.)

☀ What is the camp policy on telephone contact? When and how often can you call your child? Are there rules on campers phoning home? This is an important issue (and may come up if your child is having difficulty adjusting to camp). Some camps have a blanket rule against any telephone calls home by the campers; others permit a call home after a week at camp; still others permit unlimited telephone access. There are good reasons to support each policy, but understanding and accepting the camp policy before you enroll your child is important. You don't want to demand rule changes later.

☀ When is the camp's visiting day(s)? What is the camp program on that day? Are siblings welcome? Can the child leave the camp?

8. The bottom line

You need to ask about the total cost of the camp. This includes:

☀ transportation
☀ canteen/spending money
☀ laundry
☀ off-site trips
☀ uniforms

DEPOSIT AND FEES

You want to know how much of a deposit is required, and is it refundable? Must all camp fees be paid in full before camp begins? Ask too, what the camp's policy is if the family's plans change and they withdraw the child from the program before the start of camp or if a problem develops during camp. Is there camp fee insurance?

9. **Special requests**

   Discuss any special requests or arrangements you need to make *before* you commit to a program (and include the agreement you and the director have reached in the contract if you decide to register your child). For example, one family wanted their son to practice his violin while he was at sleepaway camp. Was the camp prepared to make sure the child had time—and was encouraged—to keep up his practice schedule? Another family wanted their daughter to practice her material for her upcoming bat mitzvah. Not only did they wonder if the time could be found, but was there anyone on staff who could help? Still another family needed to take their daughter out of camp for three days to attend a family celebration. Would there be any problem? How would they handle the logistics? Could the camp arrange for the girl to be placed on an airplane from the airport located near the camp?

   Most camps are happy to try and accommodate any special requests. If there will be a problem, you need to know ahead of time.

CHECKING REFERENCES

Part of selecting a camp should be checking references. Ask the director for names of families whose children attended the camp the previous summer. Call and ask:

☼ How did the camp handle any homesickness issues?
☼ Was the program varied and interesting?
☼ How involved was the director in the day-to-day running of the camp? If he wasn't directly involved, who was? Did that have an impact on the campers?
☼ How well supervised and interesting were any camp trips?
☼ Did their camper have any experience with the camp medical staff? Were they satisfied?

☼ Why did they choose this camp and, of course, are they planning to use it again?

☼ What age group is perfect for this camp? why?

Check with the Better Business Bureau to see if there have been any complaints registered about the camp.

Choosing a sleepaway camp can be a time-consuming process, but worth the effort to get the result that you want: a fulfilling, safe, enriching summer for your child.

Chapter 4

READY, SET, GO:
THE FUN BEGINS

I remember my sleepaway camp as the place of firsts. It was the place I first learned to use a jigsaw (I made my mother a napkin holder). It was the place I first learned to do a backward dive. It was the place I pulled my first prank (we put plastic wrap over the toilet seat in the girls' bathroom). And it was the place I had my first crush... and my first kiss.

There may be several months between the time you send in your deposit for camp and the opening day. Helping your child get ready is more than packing her trunk. You want your camper to be emotionally ready for a new adventure as well. This chapter will give you suggestions for preparing your child for camp, as well as the nitty-gritty of what needs to go to camp—*and what doesn't.*

THE DEPOSIT IS IN, RELAX

Preparing your child for camp is a delicate balance. On the one hand you want to talk about this exciting new adventure. On the other hand, you don't want to overdo the preparation. With too much discussion of the subject, camp may begin to take on mythic proportions. Your child's fantasies and expectations may never match reality, leading to disappointment. Or she can focus on her fears so much that they overwhelm her. Without the fun of daily camp life to distract her, she may focus too much on how homesick she may be. The best advice: cool it.

If there are several months before camp begins, then it might be wise to drop the subject, at least until March or April. You may begin to receive some preseason information. Some camps send a newsletter, highlighting what's planned for the upcoming summer. Others create pen pal matches between experienced campers and novices.

HOW TO TALK ABOUT CAMP

Kids have incredible radar. They will pick up *your* concerns and fears, even if you never say a discouraging word. So be careful how often and which words you choose when talking about camp.

There are lots of delightful fiction books on camp, as well as videos (see Appendix 4 for suggestions). While the story lines are often exaggerated, they can prompt discussions about how to handle camp issues. Read or watch them together.

Again, be sensitive to that fine line. Pick up on your child's subtle (and sometimes not so subtle) cues. If the books (or videos) on camp seem to be a turnoff, drop the subject. It may be overwhelming your youngster.

Most important, *never use camp as a threat or in anger.* Although at times you may feel like you really need some space between you and your child, never suggest that you're counting the days until your child is away at camp. The words can linger much longer than you intended. It also confuses him about what camp is really supposed to be. Your child should believe that camp is a fun experience and that is why you have chosen it for him.

Some Dos

Do try to have your child meet the camp director before camp begins (if only at the camp interview).

Do talk about the camp in a positive way. This lets your child know that you believe camp is a safe, exciting place for him to be.

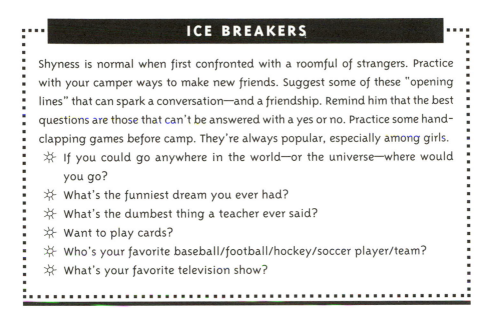

ICE BREAKERS

Shyness is normal when first confronted with a roomful of strangers. Practice with your camper ways to make new friends. Suggest some of these "opening lines" that can spark a conversation—and a friendship. Remind him that the best questions are those that can't be answered with a yes or no. Practice some hand-clapping games before camp. They're always popular, especially among girls.

☀ If you could go anywhere in the world—or the universe—where would you go?

☀ What's the funniest dream you ever had?

☀ What's the dumbest thing a teacher ever said?

☀ Want to play cards?

☀ Who's your favorite baseball/football/hockey/soccer player/team?

☀ What's your favorite television show?

Do try and arrange a play date with a fellow camper before camp begins. It helps make the transition to a new place a little easier if there is a familiar face in the bunk. If not, try and establish a link either by mail, e-mail, or phone.

Do continue to have short separations—sleepovers with friends and family. This is good practice for learning to go to sleep in an unfamiliar environment.

Do allow your child to verbalize her concerns. Even if they sound silly, she needs the emotional outlet and your reassurance. And you may learn about a worry, like a fear of darkness, that you can easily resolve (pack a flashlight).

Do talk to an experienced camper about the program. She's the perfect source for what you will really need to pack—and what you can leave at home. She can tell you what kids wear at camp and what definitely is out.

And Some Don'ts

Don't introduce anything else new in your child's life. Life should remain normal, as much as possible, at least for the opening days of camp. Although it's tempting to plan a vacation or a move when you don't have to worry about child care, your youngster may get the wrong message about why he is being sent to camp. Furthermore, it is reassuring to know that Mom and Dad, the dog and cat, his room, are where they usually are, especially during the transition to camp.

Don't try to squeeze a family vacation in just before camp starts. Plan to be at home, in your usual routine, at least five days before your child leaves for camp. He needs the comfort of his usual routine— and you'll need the time to get ready at an unhurried pace.

Don't let your child suspect your own concerns about his adjustment to camp.

GETTING READY FOR CAMP LIFE

Attending day camp helps prepare children for what a camp program will be like. But clearly sleepaway camp is fundamentally very different. At the end of the day, the camper does not return to the comfort and security of home. Nor does she have the privacy of her own house or the weekend away, to recover from an annoying run-in with a peer. At camp, she will have to deal with problems she encounters (although the counselors and staff are there to help). Furthermore, the camper has to take responsibility for her behavior, her hygiene, and belongings.

Here are some ways she can start practicing camp life at home. As you help your child develop self-reliance, you are nurturing her self-confidence and self-esteem. She'll be less fearful about her abilities to handle a new situation.

1. **Let her assume responsibility for her room and personal belongings.**
   At camp, children have the responsibility for making their own beds and cleaning up their personal area. They are in charge of their own belongings. As a group, they will be responsible for cleaning up the bunk, sweeping it out on a daily basis. Help your child learn basic housekeeping chores so that the transition to camp responsibilities is less intimidating. And it's one of the bonuses of sending your child off to camp. These life skills are transferrable to home living!

   If she is not already responsible for changing her sheets and making her own bed, now is the time to begin. Show her how to make "hospital corners."

Similarly, make sure she puts her dirty clothes in the laundry each day. While she won't have to do her own wash at camp, she will be responsible for putting it all in a bag so it can be sent out on laundry days. Similarly, have your child put her clean clothes away, much like she will have to do when she gets back her laundry and puts it away in her cubby at camp.

Review that "dirty" and "wet" are not the same thing. Make sure your child understands that towels and bathing suits need to dry before being put in the dirty clothes bag. Otherwise, with laundry collected only once a week, mildew will result as the wet pieces have time to ferment.

Taking responsibility for her belongings is an important lesson of camp. Practice putting away toys and books so she knows where they are the next time she wants or needs them. At camp, she'll need to know where her tennis racquet or soccer shoes are in order to play the game—and Mom won't be there to do a frantic search (although the counselors will, of course, try to help).

2. **Make personal hygiene a personal responsibility.** Parents often find themselves reminding their youngster about the need to brush his teeth, take a shower, wash his hair. Before he leaves for camp is the time to insist that he assume this responsibility.

If this is a struggle, make a chart, which the child will check off as he completes each of the tasks. Reserve comment or reminders until the end of each week. Review the chart together. You might even want to offer a small reward for those weeks when he accomplishes his goal.

For girls with long hair, make sure that they know how to brush it and get out the knots (pack plenty of creme rinse). If she is not already responsible for washing her own hair, now is the time to start.

One of the most popular activities during rest hour in girls' bunks is trying different hairstyles or braiding. In fact one of the skills your daughter may learn how to do at camp is "French braiding" (a more complicated, but popular hairstyle). It's tempting to suggest a haircut for the summer. Although it makes camp life easier, the transformation from Rapunzel to Sinead O'Connor can be "traumatic" for many girls and may affect how she feels about herself. It's better if your daughter practices at home how to keep her long hair manageable during camp.

> **TIP:**
> Even for girls who don't normally wear their hair in a ponytail, be sure and pack some elastic bands to tie it back. In the heat of the summer, playing active sports, girls will need to get their hair off their necks.

3. **Stay out of peer conflicts.** Learning to resolve disputes between friends is an important life lesson. As much as we would all like to ease the way for our children, it's important that they learn that *they are competent* to solve their own disagreements with friends. When your child begins to complain about a problem, or says a friend isn't being nice, don't immediately offer a solution. Let her try and figure out her options. Role play with her so she can try out various scenarios. This independence will help when she is living, 24 hours a day, in a bunk with, at least at first, strangers.

4. **Review money management.** If your child will be taking trips with the camp and will be allowed to buy souvenirs, make sure he is comfortable carrying money and counting change. When out shopping, let him pay for purchases. Instruct him how to check that he received the proper change *before* walking away from the counter. It's also helpful if you teach him to point out to the clerk the exact amount he is proffering. He might say to the sales clerk as he hands over a $10 bill: "That's $4.50 out of $10." That reduces any possible confusion over the money tendered and lessens the chance that an unscrupulous or harried cashier may take advantage of your child.

   If the camp has a canteen, you may have to deposit a certain amount at the beginning of the summer (with possible additions as the season progresses). It's possible that no money actually changes hands, but your child will still need to keep a running total of how much she is spending at the canteen. Agree on a reasonable budget (ask the director for suggestions). If your child wants more in the account, you might decide that the supplemental funds must come from her allowance. There is an educational bonus to all this money management—it's great practice at math, not to mention a wonderful life skill.

5. **Practice problem-solving skills.** There are two issues that parents must help their child learn. First, your child must learn to think

before acting. Often, when confronted with a problem, a youngster (and sometimes an adult as well) will either freeze or act impulsively. Either scenario is unhelpful. Taking time to think about what the problem is and ways in which he can resolve it is a sign of maturity.

Role play a variety of scenarios with your youngster and encourage him to come up with more than one solution to the problems you discuss. For example, ask what he would do: If he didn't like the dinner menu; if a bunk mate kept borrowing his equipment without permission; if he felt lonely; if he had a headache. While you're not trying to scare him with possible disasters he will face at camp, you do want him to know that he can often figure out, on his own, solutions to the problems he may confront. You want him to know that you have confidence in his abilities to handle camp.

But, this is the most important part of this exercise. *Make sure your child understands that he shouldn't hesitate to ask for help.* It's a sign of maturity to know that you need help. Furthermore, on a very basic level, it's the job of the counselors and staff to help campers.

Again, it's that dilemma that every parent faces. You want to teach your child independence and problem-solving skills, but you want him to understand that sometimes the best way to solve a problem is to ask for help. Before camp, ask for a list of the camp staff and review it with him. This will give him an idea of how many people are available to him as resources in camp. Let him know that he can *always* go to the camp director with a problem.

The camp director is an important resource especially if your child is having a problem with his bunk counselor. One camper was shocked and hurt when his counselor called him, in jest, by an ethnic slur. The camper finally told the director about the incident and the counselor was immediately fired. The camper's mother worried that other counselors would retaliate against her child, but the director assured her that there would be no repercussions—and there weren't. In his own staff meetings he made clear the camp's stand on that kind of behavior.

6. **Just say no!** Camp stories are often replete with the pranks pulled by and on fellow campers. Short-sheeting the counselor's bunk, toilet papering the girls' (or boys') bunk are harmless tricks that can build unity and comraderie within a group.

ESPECIALLY FOR GIRLS

Before your daughter heads off to camp for the first time, be sure and discuss menstruation, even if you think she is probably too young for it to happen during the summer. First, even if it's unlikely for her to personally experience it, other older campers (and possibly her own bunkmates) will be having their menstrual periods. She'll be more comfortable if she is at least familiar with the terms and the supplies. It's often a topic of discussion among preadolescent girls. You want her to have correct information, often to counter the myths perpetuated by other girls.

Secondly, if she does have her first period at camp, you want her to feel comfortable and unembarrassed. If you haven't packed supplies, and even if you have, suggest she go to the nurse, if only for support. One mother recalls that she took the same box of Kotex pads to camp three summers in a row. She was a late bloomer and didn't get her period until she was 14.

But at the same time, you want to be sure that your child understands that it's okay to say no—not just to drugs, tobacco, and alcohol—but also to potentially dangerous situations. Again, practice what he could say if "dared" to do something he knows would be off limits at home. You won't be able (and shouldn't try) to imagine all the possible situations, but make clear that any safety rule at camp has to be obeyed whether counselors are present or not. That means:

* no swimming without a lifeguard on duty
* never using any sports equipment without permission
* never playing with archery or riflery equipment without a counselor on duty (rope courses and gymnastic equipment are also off limits without supervision)
* no matches or lighters ever
* no wandering away from camp

But it's not only warning your child about following the crowd on a dangerous "dare," you want her to understand that peer pressure shouldn't force her to hurt another child emotionally. Hopefully the counselors will keep a close watch on the social interaction within the bunk and make sure that no child becomes the butt of too many pranks. But you want to remind your youngster to follow her own conscience in the way she treats her fellow campers.

GETTING ORGANIZED

Even before you get the suggested packing list from camp, you can begin to get organized (see the sample list, Appendix 4). Some of the requisite clothes and equipment can be purchased early and hopefully on sale. For others it would be wiser to wait until just a few months before the season begins in order to get the right size and style. While it's tempting to stock up on summer clothes at the end-of-the-season sales the previous summer, kids grow fast and unevenly. Don't buy too much because you don't know what will fit or what will be "in fashion" at the camp you've chosen.

On the other hand, the linen sales in January may be a great opportunity to stock up on the towels, blankets, and sheets your camper will need. You may prefer to raid your own linen closet for camp bedding

HAIR BUSINESS

Have your son's hair cut about a week before camp begins so it's short, but doesn't have that "just cut" look. If your son likes to keep his hair extra short (the marine haircut), he may be tempted to let friends clip it for him during the season. Advise against using "amateurs" for the cut. The camp director can arrange a visit to a local barbershop if necessary. Otherwise, it's probably better to wait until the camper returns home.

For girls, the temptation for a bunkmate to play beautician may be great, but again, the results can be a disaster. And visits to the camp's local area beauty shop may also create a problem. Unless it's strictly a trim on the bangs, suggest she wait until she comes home for a haircut. Alternatively, ask if a counselor can trim the bangs, bring scissors with you on visiting day for a quick trim, or take her to a local salon if she can leave camp and supervise the cut yourself.

supplies. See a good buy on waterproof sandals? Buy them big and put them away. The same for socks (err on the large size), a hooded poncho, a sleeping bag, sports and camping equipment.

Check It Out

The camp will send you a suggested packing list, but what's on paper and what's really needed are often two different things. The camp director will be a good resource, but an even better one is to talk directly with a family whose child was in camp the previous summer. Here you'll get the real scoop on what is a necessity, what is optional, and what the campers really wear and use. Be specific as you review the list. For example, one family dutifully packed the requisite bathrobe for their son, only to discover at this all-boys' camp, a bath towel served the same purpose when walking to and from the shower house. The bathrobe didn't make a return trip the following summer.

☼ If you've chosen a uniform camp, then you want to know if the campers wear the uniform daily while on-site, or if it is primarily for off-site trips and inter-camp games.

☼ How seriously does the camp take housekeeping chores? If the director is checking for crisp hospital corners, then you'll need to buy linens for cots. The single bed sheets you have at home are too full to produce that crisp, "bounce a quarter off the bed," look. On the other hand, if the point at camp is only to have a neat cabin, then you can use items from your own linen closet.

☼ Are many of the specialty items on the camp list, like hiking boots or thermal sleeping bags, really used? You'll need these expensive items if your camper will be taking several long hikes over tough terrain or sleeping outdoors in cool, mountainous areas. But an experienced camper from the program you've chosen can tell you whether the hikes are short, 2-mile jaunts around the lake, easily accomplished in sneakers, or something more difficult. The experienced camper can tell you if the sleeping bag your child uses for sleepovers is adequate for the camp's climate and conditions.

One camp mom advised against packing the waterproof "duck" shoes that show up on every camp list. Intended to be worn as the camper trudges across the field during rainy days, they returned in pristine condition after the first camp season. Despite several rainy days, her

> ## TIP: Better Be Color-Safe than Sorry
>
> No one is going to be separating your camper's clothes by color so be sure you send only colorfast attire and linens. Reds and dark greens and blues tend to bleed. Not only may it affect your camper's laundry, but he may be responsible for tinting an entire bunk's load of laundry! Before packing, set the color for any clothing you think might run by prewashing it in cold water. Remember that camp laundries wash in hot water.

son explained: "Who cares if your sneakers get muddy? Besides if it really bothers you, you can go barefoot."

A Word about Clothes

Some camps deliberately insist on a uniform to eliminate any competition or worry about fashion. But whatever the clothing requirements of the camp you choose may be, you want to buy durable, washable, comfortable clothing. As experienced camp moms have learned (some the hard way), sweat, dirt, and commercial laundries take their toll. While inexpensive clothes don't usually hold up to the rigors of camp life, expensive attire has no place at camp either. The emphasis is on *practical, durable, and weather sensible.*

Shrinkage: Buying the Right Size

Whatever you buy, keep in mind that camp laundries can be hard on clothes. The dirty clothes are sent to commercial laundries; there is no fine hand washing or line drying. The clothes are packed into washing machines and may be in the dryers for hours. *Shrinkage is inevitable.* Keep that in mind when buying clothes that have to last the summer. Better to err on the side of too big than too small.

The Camp Outfitter Simplifies the Task (for a Price)

There are commercial establishments that will fit your child from head to toe—and sew in the name tags to boot. (Check your yellow pages.)

These stores offer the convenience of one-stop shopping. They also provide a voice of experience. While it's still helpful to talk to an experienced camper from the program you've chosen, some of these stores have been outfitting campers for generations. They can advise on what's really a necessity at the various camps. They also know the right kind of materials that can withstand the rigors of camp, and know how to fit clothes to the child so they are still comfortable at the end of the season.

For example, Jack & Jill Youth Center in Yonkers, New York, has been a Frumkies family business since 1920, and is now the oldest camp outfitter in the nation. Sam Frumkies, the father of the current owner, explains: "Each camp has its own requirements, some too little, others excessive. A good camp outfitter can tell you where to spend money wisely and where you can save. Some camp lists are so general that they may call for things your child will never use. You have to use your common sense."

Do these services cost more? For some items, yes. If you shop carefully, you can probably save money by doing it on your own. But for those camps that insist on uniforms, you will have to order at least part of the camp list from an outfitter.

You Can Never Have Too Much Underwear or Socks

When you review the camp packing list, keep in mind the laundry cycle at the camp. You need at least a two-week supply of clothes so your child has enough to last while the clothes are in the wash. For socks and underwear, add more. Some families send as many as 24 pairs of socks, to account for those days when the camper plays hard in the morning, goes for a swim, and then needs a clean pair for the afternoon activities. Buy identical all-white socks for ease of matching. That way even if some socks are lost, your child can still make up pairs. Since it's the plaint of moms to encourage their kids to change their underwear, at least daily, pack extra so there's never the excuse of running out.

What Comes Home Doesn't Look Good

You may not recognize the clothes that return at the end of the season. Even if you get them all back—which is extremely unlikely—they will look smaller (due to shrinkage), worn out (from the high heat of the dryers), and

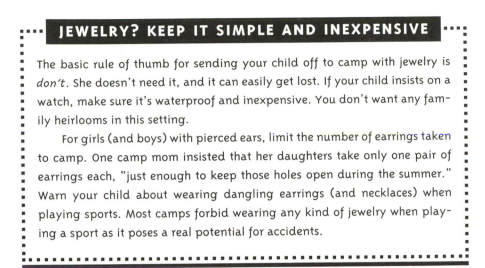

JEWELRY? KEEP IT SIMPLE AND INEXPENSIVE

The basic rule of thumb for sending your child off to camp with jewelry is *don't*. She doesn't need it, and it can easily get lost. If your child insists on a watch, make sure it's waterproof and inexpensive. You don't want any family heirlooms in this setting.

For girls (and boys) with pierced ears, limit the number of earrings taken to camp. One camp mom insisted that her daughters take only one pair of earrings each, "just enough to keep those holes open during the summer." Warn your child about wearing dangling earrings (and necklaces) when playing sports. Most camps forbid wearing any kind of jewelry when playing a sport as it poses a real potential for accidents.

may still look dirty (especially the socks). Camp life is hard on clothes. As one experienced camp mom pointed out: "I expect to get 75 percent back and at least 25 percent of that I want to throw out immediately."

On the other hand, what about those clothes or belongings that come home looking brand-new? Now you know what you don't have to pack next year!

The Scoop on Towels

Camp is heavy into water: If your child isn't sweating, he's swimming, or (hopefully) showering. While you don't want to spend a fortune on luxurious towels, the cheap, thin ones won't last or offer much absorbency. Invest in all-cotton towels, but not too heavy a weight because they will take too long to dry on the line.

Stick to standard-size bath towels. While bath sheets are luxurious and can wrap around the shivering camper, they tend to get dragged in the dirt while the camper is walking from the pool or lakeside to the cabin.

Whose Clothes Are These?

You will need to identify, either by name tape or indelible marker, every piece of clothing and equipment that you send to camp. Besides needing clear identification for laundry days, remember there will be at least eight other kids in the same bunk who have bought almost identical supplies to camp. This will help your own child remain organized and able to find her stuff.

Be sure and review with your camper *where* you are marking her name or sewing in the name tapes. Establish standard spots (on neck lapels, the back of the waist, etc.) so she can quickly identify her belongings without searching for a discreetly marked name. There's no reason why she can't write her name with indelible marker on much of her own equipment.

Sewing in name tapes is time consuming and tedious, but here are some tips that may help.

- ☼ **Skip the iron-on tapes.** Experienced campers have found that the high heat of camp laundries often loosens the glue and the iron-on tapes disappear by the end of the summer.
- ☼ **Don't be subtle.** Mark your child's name clearly and in an obvious place. You want your child to be able to pick out her belongings quickly.
- ☼ **Let someone else do the job.** If you use a camp outfitter, they may include labeling the clothes and equipment as part of the job. If not, or for those supplies you are providing yourself, you can still hire someone to do the job. Your local dry cleaner may be willing to sew in name tapes, for a fee. You could also hire a teenager: Check with your local high school home and career skills teacher (formerly known as a home economics teacher).

Keep a List of What You Send

Before you begin to fill the trunk, make a list of what you are sending and where you are packing it (if there is more than one piece of luggage). Paste the list on the inside of the trunk lid, and *keep a duplicate copy of this list at home.* That way your child will know what should be coming home at the end of the season—and should anything get lost, you'll know what you need to replace and have the information you need for insurance purposes.

How Will It Get to Camp

Each camp has its own procedure for getting the trunks, duffels, etc., to the site. The camp will send out directions. Many camps have the trunks sent ahead so they can be unpacked (by the counselors) before the campers arrive. This eases the transition to camp, but means that you have to have everything ready several days before camp starts. (It also means that you need to have enough summer clothes, underwear, swimsuits, etc., to handle those days when your camper's trunk is either enroute to or from camp.)

Sometimes, the campers will take their belongings with them on the camp bus and it all arrives at the same time. Other camps arrange for a pickup; while still others have the family ship the belongings.

Check the insurance coverage for the shipper you use. In an unfortunate incident, a camper's trunk and duffel were lost enroute to camp. Needless to say it was a poor introduction to camp life for the child. While the camp offered to replace the uniforms, etc., using the camp's outfitter, of course it took time and the child had to make do in the meantime. Furthermore, some expensive equipment was also lost. And because the family had not questioned how much insurance the shipper provided, and in retrospect realized it was inadequate, they did not take out additional coverage, which would have paid for the cost of replacing all the equipment.

The First Investment: Luggage

The camp director can give advice on what luggage (trunks, duffels, suitcases) works best for his program. In some camps the luggage is immediately unpacked and stored outside of the cabin. In that case you can choose whatever kind you prefer. But in other camps, the trunk is kept in the bunk and the camper uses it for additional storage. In that case, soft-sided luggage or duffels are less practical.

Whatever the camp prefers (or any combination), invest in sturdy materials. While there are cheaper, cardboard/pressboard trunks and nylon duffels, they don't hold up as well. The soft-sided luggage and duffels need to be heavy-duty to withstand the rigors of camp travel and life.

Some parents still have the trunks left over from their own camping days. They would swear that as compared to the more newly manufactured, "they don't make them like they used to." That may be true, but other families suggest that camp trunks are a relic from the past, heavy, awkward, and difficult to store during the winter. If you are going to use a trunk, make sure the latches and lock are well oiled and substantial. Make sure your child can open, close, lock, and unlock the trunk easily.

Other families swear by canvas duffels. They should be made of heavy canvas with strong, easily manipulated zippers. Your camper may be responsible for packing much, if not all of her belongings by herself at the end of the season. Will she be able to close the luggage easily—and will it withstand the tugging and pulling, as she stuffs them with a season's worth of belongings and memories?

THE UNWRITTEN ESSENTIALS

From the list your camp provides and from discussions you'll have with the director and other campers, you'll discover the clothes and equipment you'll need to send. But there are other essentials that may not show up on any official list that can smooth the transition in the opening days of camp, as well as offer the comfort and security of home over the length of the camper's stay.

Comfort Items While you can't pack your child's bedroom and ship it off, be sure and include some favorite stuffed animals. Although it is undoubtedly gender stereotyping, girls have it easier in bringing comfort objects from home. The first-time boy camper may be hesitant to include his stuffed bear. Again, check with other families of experienced campers. Undoubtedly you'll find that other boys do include their favorite stuffed animal. But if he's still unsure, consider sending a favorite pillowcase or comforter. A picture of the family, including the dog, cat, or even goldfish, can also be reassuring—even if consigned to the bottom of the trunk. Several camp moms said that their sons always had their comfort items with them—their thumbs!

A First Letter Be sure and include a short message that your camper will find when she opens the trunk and unpacks. While you should send a letter to camp before she leaves (see chapter 5 for staying in touch), including a *short* note in with her belongings guarantees that she will have mail as soon as she arrives. Keep the note brief and upbeat. If you want, include a comic book or something else that she can share with her new bunkmates.

Dear Maggie,

I'm thinking about your first dip in the pool. I bet it will be refreshing after the long bus ride.

Here's a riddle for you.

What is the beginning of eternity?
The end of time and space?
The beginning of every end?
(turn over the paper for the answer)

Have fun,
Love, Mom

(answer: the letter "e")

A Deck of Cards This is a bunk staple. Your child will enjoy playing games with friends during rest hour—and even may enjoy a game of solitaire on her own. Pack two decks so more can play (and a complete deck is always available if some get lost).

A Flashlight You may want to include more than one kind. Pack the traditional handheld variety, but also include a "miner's lamp" flashlight as well. These are perfect for reading in bed when the lights are out.

Books Camp is no place for *War and Peace* (unless you have the unusual child). But kids do enjoy reading during rest hour and in bed before going to sleep. The popular series books are always easy reads and can be shared by bunkmates. You might also pack magazines and game/puzzle books.

Games The travel-size version of the popular games are great fun and terrific icebreakers for kids. They provide your child with a "hook" for making a connection with other campers. Don't pack too many or anything with too many parts (there's not much room in most bunks and small parts are easily lost). Camps always have plenty of regulation-size board games for rainy days. A piece of string to play "cat's cradle" etc., may be old-fashioned, but is still popular.

Cassette/Disc Player with Headphones Kids enjoy listening to music and books on tape. Others use music tapes as a way to go to sleep. Some families record a message and send "letters on tape" to their camper.

Send an Inexpensive Model Equipment gets lost, unfortunately sometimes stolen, and certainly can get broken at camp.

Batteries   One camp mom has said you can never have too much under-wear, socks, or batteries! The kids will need lots of batteries, especially if they forget to turn off the cassette player or flashlight.

Disposable Camera   This is a great way for your child to capture her camp life and share it with the family at home. Taking pictures of fun events is a good habit to get into, a wonderful life skill, and a great icebreaker for the shy child.

Yearbook   Kids may want to pack their school yearbook or make their own. Again, it's a way for children to get to know each other and share their two worlds. If your child is making her own pre-camp scrapbook, make sure she includes family and friends pictures, pet photos, and special mementoes she wants to share with others.

Autographs Please   Kids enjoy having an autograph book or stuffed animal that new friends can sign with an indelible pen. Bibi Schweitzer, thirteen-year-old author of *Avoiding Homesickness: Surefire Ways to Beat the Sleepaway Camp Blues* (see Appendix 5 for how to order), has a novel approach to the autographable item. She recommends taking an oversize T-shirt and indelible pen to camp. Fellow campers can sign the shirt and your child will have a permanent, wearable memento.

Stationery, Pens, Stamps, Address Book   Some kids are natural born corre-spondents, and certainly homesick campers can be prolific writers. In any case, pack some stationery and pre-addressed, stamped envelopes to make sure that you get at least a weekly missive from camp (most coun-selors try to enforce the rule of once a week a letter to home). Help your camper make an address book of family and friends. Remind her that she's more likely to get a letter if she writes one!

SCHEDULE A MEDICAL CHECKUP

June is a busy month for pediatricians as they try to fit in all the medical checkups for campers about to depart for the summer. Avoid the rush and schedule your child's checkup in April or May. Even if you don't have the camp's medical forms yet, you can still schedule the appointment and send the forms in for completion when they arrive.

Don't forget to include a dental checkup as well—and have any nec-essary work done before camp.

Here are some other issues to discuss with your child's doctor.

* **Vaccination alert** Double-check that your child is fully immunized. Is her tetanus shot still current?
* **Medications** If your child already takes medication on a routine basis, make sure you have: a current prescription (which you can send to camp with the medical forms); the instructions from your doctor as to dosage; an adequate supply of the medication. Discuss with your doctor whether your child can take a summer "holiday" from medication—but *do not make this decision without consulting with your medical caregiver*. Children who are on antidepressants, antipsychotics, or other psychiatric medications should continue taking them. Reassure your child that the medical staff is discreet and there are many children at camp who need to take a variety of medications.
* **Allergies** If your child already suffers from seasonal allergies, ask if your child should change or add to his medications to deal with being in a camp environment.
* **Personal responsibility** Although the camp will have a strong on-site medical staff, remind your camper that he too must assume some responsibility for taking care of himself. Many camps accept children who suffer from, but have under control, a chronic illness, such as asthma or diabetes. Unfortunately, kids will sometimes see camp as a way to escape dealing with the illness. As one camp doctor recalled: "We had an asthmatic 13-year-old who would refuse to stop any athletics despite severe wheezing. When we forced him to sit out, he complained. He was away from home where he no longer had to listen to his parents so he figured he could get away with playing while wheezing."
* **Don't rely on forms** Although you will provide the camp with the necessary medical forms and information, ask to speak directly to your camper's counselor, as well as the medical staff if your child has a potentially life-threatening illness or condition. For example, one mother whose son suffers from a severe nut allergy (the child develops an anaphylactic reaction if he ingests nuts), spoke to the camp nurse, dietician, head counselor, and group counselors about her son's condition. She was glad she did when it was a counselor who read the ingredient list on the potato chips bag and noticed that the chips were cooked in peanut oil!
* **Insect repellant and waterproof sunscreen** Be sure and pack both in your camper's bag, but even more important, review with your child the need to use both on a regular basis. Sunscreens, even those with

a high SPF level, only delay sunburn, not prevent it, so extended exposure to the sun, even if your camper has used sunscreen, can still result in sunburn. That's why it's important to remind your camper to wear hats and shirts (for the highly sun sensitive, wear a T-shirt while swimming). On those days when your camper is around the water for an extended period (for example, on a canoe trip), urge her to apply a sunblock, like zinc oxide, on her nose and cheeks.

☼ **Glasses** Invest in a second set and send both to camp. You may also want to buy sports safety glasses. Include your child's prescription for glasses with the medical forms.

☼ **Check with the orthodontist** Many camps can arrange for emergency or even routine orthodontia treatment. Ask your child's orthodontist if treatment can wait until after camp, or does your child need to be seen and braces adjusted during the season. If treatment is required, can the camp's dental professionals handle the visit? Have your orthodontist write a list of instructions to send to camp. Be sure and pack your child's orthodontia materials (for example, rubber bands, retainer).

OFF TO CAMP

After months of searching, decision-making, preparation, and packing, it's finally the night before your child leaves for camp.

Get Organized

You want to avoid mini-disasters in the morning, so lay out what you and your child *both* agree she will wear in the morning. Again, the emphasis is on *comfort*, both physically and psychologically. If you have bought your youngster a new outfit for the first day of camp, make sure to wash it to rid it of any stiffness. Similarly, make sure that new shoes are "broken in."

If you have any additional paperwork you must provide the camp, place it in an envelope with your child's name on the outside, so that you can bring it with you in the morning. Put all camp supplies by the door (and perhaps a camera for opening day photos) so that you don't have to search for last-minute items in the morning.

If possible, try to keep the night before leaving for camp, a quiet evening—no friends sleeping over. You want your child to be rested before his big adventure begins. Try to keep to his regular bedtime, and if necessary, linger a few minutes for last-minute reassurance.

> **TIP:**
> Try to arrive early at the camp pickup so that you or your child don't feel rushed in your good-byes.

In the Morning

Build a few extra minutes into your schedule to allow for the unexpected.

Even if your child is very excited (or nervous), try to encourage her to eat a balanced breakfast. Skip the sugar cereals, and go for a nutritious meal that will provide her with a morning full of energy. (Besides most camps offer a wide variety of sugar cereals for breakfast, as well as more nutritious choices, so let that be the camp treat!) But this is no time for a food fight. What you are trying to do is make the morning as easy and stress-free as possible.

If she has a long bus ride ahead and tends to suffer from motion sickness, check with your doctor about when and how much anti-nausea medication you should give before she boards the bus. Be sure and tell the bus counselor if you've given your child any medication.

Make It Short and Sweet

The moment has arrived. It's time to leave. The best case scenario is a warm, quick hug, a few words of love, and then good-bye. This is not the moment for any long reflections on what it all means. It's better if you can stave off the tears until you are alone. Your child may be fighting to keep himself together and may not be able to sustain it if he sees you cry.

On the other hand, if you fall apart—and it has happened to many people—that's okay too. You'll all survive, and while you may be momentarily embarrassed, this too shall pass. It's one of those stories that your child will understand better when he has kids of his own.

Suppose She Cries

"My daughter tried to keep it together, but she looked like she did when she was three years old and I left her at nursery school for the first time. She started to cry. Luckily a counselor came over, put her arms around my daughter, and encouraged her to give me a kiss and get on the bus.

Turns out my child really did love camp, but my first inclination that day was to grab my daughter and put her back in our car and go home."

It's natural to want to protect your child from any kind of hurt and it's especially hard when you empathize with their fears and concerns. If she does start to cry, remind your child that:

☼ you know it's hard to separate

☼ you understand that it can be scary to try something new

☼ but that you also are sure that she is ready for this new adventure and that she'll have a wonderful time at the camp you both have carefully chosen.

You really can't prolong this conversation—it's not beneficial for your child or you. Ask one of the camp counselors to help your child get on the bus.

This can be one of the most difficult moments of parenting—maintaining your confidence that this adventure will be a fun, educational experience in the face of a tear-stained face.

Try to remember that separation may be difficult, but just like she grew to love preschool and thrived as she gained confidence in her own abilities, going to camp will provide your child with new opportunities for growth. At the moment when you say good-bye, it may appear to be a leap of faith, but rest assured, good camp programs are prepared to help children overcome homesickness. They've seen it and done it so they are ready, willing, and able to make sure your child enjoys this new experience.

Once your camper arrives on-site, the fun begins. In the next chapter you'll find tips for keeping in touch, dealing with homesickness (at a distance), visiting day, and what to do when and if problems arise.

Chapter **5**

KEEPING IN TOUCH:
SHARING THE FUN

*Last summer my husband and I celebrated our 20th anniversary
with a two-week vacation in Europe. Even though my daughter was
13 years old and had been going to sleepaway camp for four years,
I still worried about how she would feel if she didn't get mail every
few days. But I couldn't guarantee the mail delivery from overseas.
So I made up four care packages, filled with the usual stuff I send
her at camp, nail polish, magazines, puzzle books, along with little notes, and then had my next door neighbor send one to the
camp every three days. Crazy? I know. But my daughter actually
thanked me!*

Keeping in touch with your camper starts before she boards the bus and
continues throughout the weeks that she is away. It's more than cards,
letters, and care packages—although they are essential. *What you say
and how you respond to what your child is telling you* about camp life is
critical to her adjustment to this new adventure. In this chapter we'll talk
about homesickness: what it is, what it isn't, and how to help your child.
We'll give you *parent-tested* strategies for coping. We'll also cover how
to work with the camp administration to make sure that everyone is
working *together* to support your camper.

The letters you write, the packages you send, and the telephone conversations (if permitted) will be your primary links to camp. Here's how to make them caring, effective, and fun.

Visiting Day at camp is a special opportunity for your child to share her new life. Here's what to expect and the best way to make it a happy day for all.

And if you get that phone call from camp telling you your child is ill, here's what you need to ask and if necessary, do.

SHE'S ON THE BUS: NOW WHAT?

Sending your child off to camp for the first time may provoke a range of parental emotions. You may be proud, excited, and happy. If you have been at home with your child, you may also feel relief at the thought of a few weeks of freedom. And you may feel guilt that you feel that way. You may worry that your child isn't ready for camp. You may feel depressed that your child is getting older, less dependent on you. This marks a new stage in his life and yours. You may feel all, some, or none of these emotions—and you may feel them at the same time or successively. It's all very *normal* to have any of these feelings. And it is just as normal if you don't.

What Your Child May Be Feeling

In the weeks before camp starts, your child may also be experiencing a myriad of emotions. She may be excited, confused, worried, even bewildered. You need to recognize that it would be perfectly reasonable for any child to be both excited *and* worried about a strange place everyone keeps insisting will be a lot of fun, but at the same time, does not provide the stability and comfort of what she already knows. It's normal for a child to feel that camp is both thrilling and a little scary—like any brand-new experience.

Homesickness: What Is It?

You don't have to be a camper to suffer from homesickness. Consider how you would feel if you were asked to go to a place full of strangers, in a place you had never visited before (or only briefly). Or suppose you went on a business trip and were told that you had to share a room with six or more complete strangers—for weeks. Wouldn't you miss home, even if you did like this new, exciting place?

Separation anxiety is a normal part of childhood. It is not only developmentally appropriate, but actually essential. Research has shown that this same attachment, formed in the first year of a baby's life, is the foundation for a healthy emotional development in adults. The loving, trusting relationship that an infant develops with his parents teaches the child that the adult world can be counted on to provide him with his basic needs.

The flip side of attachment is, of course, separation. And that can be scary for children (and adults). But just as an infant learns that his mother will come from behind her hands and reappear when they play a game of peekaboo, it's part of a child's emotional development to learn to trust that he can go away and his parents and life will be there when he returns. A camper *intellectually* knows that separation is followed by reunion, but emotionally it may be difficult to accept.

But in the midst of coping with adjusting to living with strangers in a new environment, children can get overwhelmed. Unlike the separation anxiety your child may have experienced when she started preschool, there is no return at the end of the day to the familiarity of home. So there is no break in the stress of adjusting. Homesickness is a perfectly normal reaction. Even for children who enjoy new adventures, delight in sleepovers at friends and relatives, a bout of homesickness is a common reaction.

What Homesickness Is Not

It's important not to measure your success as a parent by your child's adjustment to camp. If your youngster has a difficult time adjusting to camp, it doesn't mean that somehow you failed to create an independent child.

Nor should you wonder *why* the hysteria at going to camp. At times it's almost as if your youngster believes he will never see you again. As one mother wondered, "I was amazed at how difficult my daughter found the first weeks at camp. She wrote us these tragic letters, confiding that she was crying herself to sleep every night. It's not as though she had never been away from home before. What happened?" First of all, put it in context. Your child may not be looking for a logical response from you.

This is a situation when all she needs is *comfort and reassurance.* There are times when a child can't respond to reason. Remember, when adults are very anxious, they don't always act logically or respond to reason either!

Homesickness is not about your child loving or trusting you enough. Nor is it about his independence or willingness to take risks. It's a temporary situation that, with the support of adults, he can overcome. And when he does, it will be an enormous boost to his self-confidence and self-esteem.

So Why Isn't He Crying?

It's equally important not to feel upset or worried if your child sails through camp with nary a backward glance. It doesn't mean you failed to develop a strong attachment to your child, nor that he doesn't love you enough to care whether he's home or not. If your child handles separation well, enjoy it.

In the parenting worry sweepstakes, consider that you won on this issue, but there will be plenty of other occasions for you to worry!

Who Will Cry

Since separation is about change, it's not surprising that it affects some children more than others. You probably already know if your youngster adapts easily to change or is more likely to suffer a strong case of the homesickness blues.

☼ How does he react to new situations?
☼ Does he readily try new foods?
☼ Is his bedtime routine fixed in cement?
☼ Is he shy around other children?

It's not that this type of child won't adjust to camp, it's just that it may take a little more patience and reassurance as he adapts to this change in his life. Some children adjust to change more easily than others. It's not something to worry about, but it helps to be realistic about your child's general response to change. Knowing that he often has problems adjusting to new situations allows you to be realistic about what the opening weeks of camp will be like. You'll be ready to help him successfully cope with the adjustment.

DON'T BE AFRAID OF CRYING

Camp directors uniformly agree that in many ways, it's preferable to deal with a child who is up front about his unhappiness and cries, rather than face the quiet child who retreats and is withdrawn. His unhappiness may be deeper and may be missed. While no parent wants to hear that his child is unhappy and crying, take comfort that your child is willing to share with other adults that he is having difficulty. *Parents must understand and need to make clear to their kids that asking for help is a sign of maturity.*

Unexpected or Delayed Problems

Sometimes parents are surprised that their youngster is having trouble separating. She may have had a sitter since birth and never appeared troubled when Mom or Dad left. Remember that you are putting your child not only on "foreign" turf, but with a new set of adults. She has none of the "comforts" of home base. That is why carrying some security item with her to camp can ease the transition.

Sometimes a child will enter camp and for the first few days suffer no problems. Then for some reason, she may be hit by a wave of homesickness. It may be the novelty of camp has worn off and the child can now focus on separation. It's frustrating, but generally these brief bouts of homesickness pass quickly with the patience and reassurance of staff and parents.

Post-Visiting Day Meltdown

It's not unusual for a child to have problems separating after Visiting Day. Again, as your child plunges back into the daily routines of camp and is once again swept up in the excitement of the program, the anxiety will pass.

Or some children have problems following a phone call from home. At one camp, where the policy was to permit a telephone call home *after* the first week, one boy became very upset following the conversation. He finally asked his counselor to call his parents again and explain that it was just too hard talking on the telephone. He could handle the separation, he actually was thoroughly enjoying camp, but couldn't handle the homesickness he felt following the telephone calls. In this case, the parents respected their child's judgment (and in fact, the youngster continued to return to the camp for the next seven years, finally serving as a counselor). *You have to do what works for your child.*

Parental Anxiety

Sending your child off to camp can be traumatic for parents as well. It can trigger an emotional response to think that one stage of childhood, at least with this offspring, is behind you. One mother felt very foolish when she came home from leaving her youngest child and his siblings off at camp and promptly burst into tears. For this woman, it was the first time in 11 years that she and her husband would be home alone. It was the end of one phase of parenting, and while there were still many years of family work ahead, there was sadness at the end of this period.

Children can be incredibly perceptive. Unconsciously, parents sometimes transfer their feelings of sadness or uncertainty about camp to their children. Watch those vibes!

The Preemptive Strike against Homesickness

Just as you discuss other camp issues, it's important to be up front about homesickness. What you are doing is giving your child *permission* to feel homesick. He needs to know that it's a normal emotion, and that even if homesick, he can still have a good time.

- ☼ Before your child leaves for camp, acknowledge that homesickness is a common, normal reaction.
- ☼ Remind your child that you are confident that even though she may miss you, she will still be able to enjoy the camp experience.
- ☼ Encourage her to share her emotions with her counselors and the camp director.
- ☼ *It's equally important that she doesn't worry about you.* You don't want your child to feel responsible for making you happy or filling your days. One boy, the oldest in his family, actually told his mother that what he loved about camp was that he didn't have to "worry" about his family when he was there.

On the other hand, it's a fine line you walk. While you want to be prepared to help your child should he have a problem, you certainly don't want to act as if you *expect* a problem. If you hover too much, or over-prepare your youngster, you may undermine your child's self-confidence. The message you may be sending is: "Camp is a place where you will be unhappy *and* you won't be able to cope with your sadness." You could end up creating a problem where one didn't exist. It's the tightrope act that parents have to walk frequently.

Vaccinate against Homesickness

While you may not be able to eliminate all homesickness, you can *immunize* your camper to a certain extent *before* she leaves home.

Role Play Adults and children both cope better when they know what to expect in a new situation. So besides talking about camp, *practice some of the new situations*. While you obviously can't anticipate them all, there are some scenarios you can role play at home. For example, if the camp bathrooms are outside the bunks, have your child practice with a flashlight finding an object in the backyard at night. It's a little thing, but it gives your child a preview of what to expect and how he really is capable of handling this new situation.

Welcome to Camp Besides the letter you include in his camp trunk when he arrives, send letters to your child at camp a few days before he leaves so he will find mail when he arrives. Try and write every day so he will have a steady stream of cards and letters at each mail call. Again, those opening days of camp are when he is most vulnerable. You don't want him to feel like he is the only one in his bunk who didn't receive mail.

Put the Camp on Notice If you have reason to suspect that your child may have difficulty adjusting, talk it over with the director *before* your child arrives at camp. That way the director can keep a special eye out for any signs of problems. After the first day or two of camp, check with the director. Even if there is a no telephone rule for the campers, it doesn't mean that you can't be in touch with the administration. By calling, you'll probably get the reassurance you need that your child is doing fine, although perhaps feeling somewhat homesick. *Expect that.*

Check that Your Mail Is Arriving If there is a problem with the mail delivery, ask if you can fax a letter to your child immediately.

He's Homesick: Now What?

You anticipated it, but it still hurts when you get the letter from camp, with teardrops he's circled on the paper, telling you that he's having the worst time of his life, misses you terribly, and wants to come home, *immediately*.

Now what?

While it's understandable that you may panic and rush to the rescue, *stop*. The best thing you can do for your child is to reach for the telephone and call the camp director. Here's where your careful pre-camp planning pays off. Take comfort that you have chosen a director you believe understands children, is experienced dealing with these situations, and is looking to help you help your child succeed. Your child is not facing this tough experience alone.

Sometimes a parent's call to the director is the first notice that the child is having problems. This doesn't mean that the director is insensitive or uninvolved. There are several possibilities: Your child is masking his homesickness; he's not as intensely homesick as the letter would lead you to believe so the bunk counselors have been able to cope without involving the director; or the intense emotions that prompted the tragic letter home have passed.

Tell the director about the letter and your concerns. You want him to investigate the situation and then report back to you, *that same day*. A good director will not whitewash the situation, but at the same time, he should be able to put it in perspective. He should be experienced enough to know when the situation is typical homesickness and when it's not.

The director should also be prepared to tell you what they are doing at camp to ease the situation for your child. The best plan, of course, is for your child to be kept busy and involved in activities. As the youngster gets wrapped up in the camp program, she'll be too busy to focus on being homesick and too tired at night to stay awake and worry. Camp friendships will also help.

The director should talk directly with your child, as well as with the bunk staff. The director should then report back to you *specifics* about what is being done—and agree to talk again in a day or two to update the situation.

As one camp director explained: "It is my opinion that a parent who has chosen a particular camp did so because they felt comfortable with the camp, its program, and its people. You have to trust your camp director. Don't blindly follow his or her advice without question, but DO NOT PANIC. The strong feeling we get from parents at this point is 'we don't want him to hate us because we made him stay.' Trust me, no camp director wants a camper to hate him or her either. And a parent will often think a director is just scared he will have to refund tuition. Almost certainly, a parent signed a no-refund policy anyway so the camp director has no incentive to keep the child there other than his belief in the growth that comes from overcoming a challenging experience. A homesick camper is disruptive and time consuming, so sending him or her home would be an easy option for the camp."

GENDER DIFFERENCES

It's not surprising that in a recent study of how children cope with home-sickness, boys and girls experience it in equal measure, but girls are more open about their emotions. Girls tend to talk it over with a friend or coun-selors, while boys tend to keep their emotions private. This can make it more difficult for a boy. Remind your son that it's a sign of maturity to ask for help.

Guilt Appeal

One first-time camper, age eight, was blunt with her mom. "If you're *really* my mother, you'll come and get me immediately." Well that pretty neatly summarizes every parent's worst fear! The phone call from camp that challenges you with raw emotion.

Now 20, the camper turned counselor looks back and laughs at the dramatics, but can still recall the passions of the moment. Yes, to a certain extent, she did feel abandoned. Yes, she was angry, especially with her father who insisted that she stay at camp (Mom was more willing to forget the whole thing). And most of all, yes she is glad that her parents made her stay because she ended up loving the place, she felt good about her ability to cope, and in fact returned for eight more years to the same camp, eventually serving as counselor.

Here's what this former camper knows (albeit in retrospect). Her parents were calling the director frequently in the opening days of camp asking questions like: Is she smiling; is she participating; is she eating; has she made friends; is she grooming herself? Parents and director were working together to make sure that this was just another transient case of homesickness. One that with support and resolve could be handled so that the camper could get down to the business of enjoying herself. To the camper, the message from her parents was clear:

☼ we're sorry you're sad;
☼ we believe that you will enjoy this experience in a few days;
☼ we want you to stay at camp;
☼ everyone at camp wants to help you succeed, and
☼ let's discuss this again in another week.

What's the Game Plan?

This is the most difficult part: Parents need to be in agreement that they will hang tough in their decision that the child will complete her stay at camp.

The first leap of faith you make is that you must trust the judgment of the director who's on site and can see first hand what is happening to your child. You must believe that the director will put your child's situation in perspective based on years of experience.

What to do? It depends in part on the rules and policies of the camp. If you have chosen a camp that has a "no telephone calls with campers' rule," then you must abide by it now.

But rules and reality aren't always the same. Although some camps may technically have a "no-phone" rule, directors often use their own discretion about when to bend it. As one camp director admitted: "While we officially don't permit campers to phone home, it's really a matter of judgment—my judgment. Sometimes, when I think it will help, I call the parents ahead of time, get their agreement that we all believe and will tell the child that he should stay at camp, and then have the camper call home. But only if I believe that we're all on the same page as to what is the best course of action. It doesn't help the camper if he's getting conflicting messages from home and camp. Frankly, when I've thought it would help a child get through a tough adjustment period, I've had the camper call home several times. I have to use my judgment about what will work best with each child."

But if the rule at the camp is no telephone calls, you shouldn't insist on talking to your child after receiving a sad letter from camp. And the truth is that you knew what the telephone policy was before you sent your child to camp and discussed it with him and the director before enrolling (see chapter 2). So both parent and child should have been comfortable about the policy before signing up—and demanding that the policy be changed now may only confuse your youngster. The camper may think "if that decision can change, perhaps we can rethink the whole idea of camp?"

When pushed by parents to speak to their child, one director is blunt: "I tell parents 'if I think it will help then I will put him on the phone but are you strong enough to say what we agreed?' If I do not feel it will help I will not put the child on the phone. It is a pure gut feeling. If a parent insists, I will tell them that I will call the child to the phone, but that they should be prepared to come and pick him or her up because at that point I feel I have lost the parent's confidence and the child will almost certainly be unable to go back and function as a member of his group. This last scenario almost never happens, maybe once every two or three years."

If you do speak on the telephone, even if your child cries, you must remain calm. Here are some do's and don'ts.

DO

Do make it clear that you understand and sympathize with her feelings.

Do encourage her to continue to express her emotions to you in letters.

Do advise her to share her feelings with the camp staff.

Do stress that you have confidence in her ability to stay at camp and have a good time.

Do point out that you believe that the camp staff will help her through this tough time.

Do remind her that you made this decision about camp together and that she made a commitment to stay at camp.

Do review the coping techniques you had discussed before she left for camp.

DON'TS

Don't remind her about how much money the camp costs.

Don't embarrass or ridicule her by suggesting that this is babyish behavior.

Don't compare her to her siblings or friends.

Don't suggest that she ignore her feelings or that she is being over-dramatic.

If you can't have a telephone conversation, then you must convey these thoughts in a letter. Explain that you are in touch with the camp staff, that you both agreed to abide by the telephone rule, but that you are working with the camp staff to help her succeed, and will be talking to the camp director regularly to check on her progress.

You might also try to put the situation in perspective. Try to get her to see just how short a time period you are really talking about. For example, point out that the child goes to school for 10 months of the year—and this is only one month! Some kids find it helpful to keep a journal. It might help her if she can write down how she is feeling—and can see for herself if she is making progress in adjusting.

WHEN TO CALL IT QUITS

Is it ever right to say this just isn't working and bring your child home? Sure, but it's a decision that should be made with a great deal of thought and awareness of the long-term consequences. Campers who do come home before the end of their stay often feel like failures. Even those who don't like the camp for programmatic reasons, still feel a sense of accomplishment if they can handle the separation and last through the expected time period.

Sometimes, even with the best of intentions on the part of the parents and staff, however, a child is just not ready for camp or it's just not a good fit. If after a real trial, and the best efforts and teamwork between home and camp, the child is clearly not adjusting, it's time to bring the camper home. As one director explained: "It's not a prison. When the child is getting physically sick, throwing up everyday from crying, and we've made a real effort, in concert with the parents, to help the youngster adjust and it just isn't working, then it's time to consider sending the camper home."

And the problem child who needs to go home is not just the youngster who is not eating, is withdrawn, and refuses to be engaged in the camp activities. Sometimes a child acts out, runs away, hurts others, himself, or property, who is sending the clear message that he needs to go home. One camp director said these kinds of behavior problems usually result when the child believes that he had no role in making the decision about going to camp.

If you make the decision to bring your child home, hopefully in concert with the camp staff, then you need to support your child through what may be perceived as a failure. You don't want to go through an intense reevaluation the day he comes home, but after a few days, you do want to sort through what went right (and there must have been some things) and what went wrong with this experience. *You want your child to understand that while the camp experience was disappointing, he is not a failure because he came home.* You also want to suggest that perhaps you will reconsider another sleepaway camp program at another time because you have confidence in his abilities.

KEEPING IN TOUCH

Cards, letters, and care packages help children adjust to camp. These bridges between home and camp are a source of comfort, as well as a means of reaching out and connecting to bunkmates.

The Perfect Camp Letter

Writing those first camp letters is a tricky business. You want to convey to your child that you love and miss him, but you don't want to overdo it so he is awash in guilt and homesickness. You want to tell him about what's happening at home, but you don't want to make it sound like so much fun that he wishes he were there instead of at camp. So what can you talk about?

Like any good letter writer, you should first ask about what's happening *there.* And because you have a good idea about what daily camp life is like from your pre-camp meeting(s) with the director, you can ask *specifics,* for example about the waterfront (*Have you tried waterskiing? How was the swim test?*); the meals (*How were the special waffles they told us about? What are the desserts?*); the arts and crafts (*What woodworking project are you making?*), etc.

You can then talk about what is happening on the home front. Frankly, most of the time our lives aren't that interesting, so look for anecdotes about friends, the neighborhood, the town. Remember, you want to make a connection between home and camp, but you don't want to make it seem that all the good stuff started happening at home the day he walked out the door!

Yes, you can even talk about the weather (tell her how it's beastly hot, especially if you know that it will be nicer at camp); how the town pool was closed for repairs; progress on the family vacation plans when your camper comes home.

The letter doesn't have to be long. In this case, quantity, a letter every day or two, is better than quality. Although one seasoned camper, after receiving a letter every day from his mother for three camp seasons, finally wrote back and said: "Stop, you don't have to write every day." Here are some parent-proven letter writing tips.

When You Care Enough. . . . Alternate your letters with funny greeting cards.

Include a Joke, Riddle, Puzzle, News Clippings This gives your camper an icebreaker with her bunkmates. One mom included the sports stats in her letters to camp; another sent funny newspaper cartoons.

Limit Criticism If a report card appears after a child has left for camp; if his room was left a mess; if you discover an old sandwich under the bed—save the discussion for when the camper comes home. It's hard to have a meaningful dialogue on paper.

Pre-Address Envelopes Most camps have a rule about writing home at least once a week. Make it easy for your camper to send you a letter by providing postcards or envelopes pre-addressed home or to grandparents.

Make Writing Fun If your camper is likely to be a letter writer (often girls enjoy correspondence), include a fun stationery pack (either homemade or store bought). Look for jazzy writing paper, a pen with multicolored ink, stickers, etc. Develop an address book that includes the camp addresses of friends.

No Grammar or Spell Check Absolutely never comment on writing, spelling, or grammatical errors in your child's letters.

Be Realistic Remember that your camper may not write much; may not write well; and may not write often. Keep in mind that the point of camp was for him to immerse himself in the experience, not develop a lengthy, intense correspondence with you. If he isn't writing, and the word from camp is that all is well, then take comfort that he is too busy having fun to pen letters home.

Stay in Touch Ignore his correspondence abilities, and continue to write, even if you get one line or no letters in return. It will make your camper—and you—feel better.

When the News Is Bad

Sometimes you'll have some unfortunate news you need to share with your camper. Before you write a letter detailing the problems, consider how important it is to share the information at this point, or whether it could wait until she returns home. For example, if there has been an accident in town; if you or your partner has lost his job; if the family pet is ill, you might prefer to wait until you can discuss the issues face-to-face.

But if it's an emergency, for example, a close family member has died or is very ill and you believe your child needs to know, call and talk it over first with the director. You want to make sure that there is an adult from whom your camper can receive the emotional support he may need to handle the news. Furthermore, you want to discuss with the director what you want to do next. Do you want to bring your child home permanently or temporarily? Many camps permit children to go home for an emergency and then return.

And it may be that the best thing for your child is to come home and then return to camp. One family brought their daughter home for the funeral of a great-grandmother. Following the services, the child returned to camp. The camp director can help you assess your child's emotional health and offer support if she returns to the program.

Care Packages That Show You Care

Camp care packages are always welcome, but make sure you know what is permitted at the camp. Some programs strictly enforce no-food-permitted rules, requiring that children open the packages in front of the camp staff. There's a good reason for this regulation as one camper ruefully discovered. Artfully hiding some forbidden candy in her shoes under her bunk, the camper was disgusted to find an ant invasion of her shoes, clothes, even her bedding! Other camps do permit food from home, although be sure and include a tight container to prevent an animal/bug infestation.

Other good care packages include comic books (great for sharing), books, stickers, crazy hats, nail polish, stick-on earrings, googly eyes—generally any toy that you might include in a party loot bag. You might send decorations, barrettes, or T-shirts to help celebrate the Fourth of July. Your camper may have requests for clothing or accessories for a talent night or scavenger hunt, or need additional batteries. Sometimes the camper will request something that you know is available in the canteen (shampoo, toothpaste, toothbrush). He may know it too, but doesn't want to spend his money on necessities. Or sometimes, as one camper wistfully pointed out: "Buying it at the canteen is not the same as a care package."

Telephone Connections

Many camps have a no-telephone-call rule or variations of it. Some permit no calls home during the summer; others permit one call home after the first 10 days; still others allow telephone calls on the child's birthday or the birthday of a parent. You and your camper must understand clearly what the rules are *before* she leaves for camp. It will be easier for all if the expectations about telephone communication are clear.

The problem with telephone calls home, says one counselor, is that "parents are confronted with the emotion of the moment and can't put it in context. If you get a letter saying: 'I hate this place, take me home,' a parent can call camp and get a fuller explanation from me [the counselor]. I might say, 'Yes, your son was having a bad day when he wrote that letter, but he's fine now.' But with a telephone call, all you get is the emotion the kid is feeling right that minute—and some of it may be a result of hearing the parent's voice. You don't get the counselor's or director's perspective of what's happening to your kid on a typical camp day."

Furthermore, some kids aren't great conversationalists, either in person or on the phone, so the discussion may be somewhat limited or forced. As one mother confessed, "I felt sort of like a prosecutor, asking a million questions, and basically getting yes and no answers. But to be honest, that's the kind of conversations we have when he's home."

You know your child, and you know whether telephone calls home will be helpful or not, informative or merely touching base. If telephone calls are permitted, here are some tips for making them reassuring to the camper and productive for you.

1. **Keep it short** Three minutes is more than enough time to touch base with your camper and get the list of what your child wants you to bring on Visiting Day. Most camps have a time limit on these calls: respect it.

2. **Keep it light** It's fine to say you love and miss your child, but you don't want the conversation to become maudlin—or to touch off a bout of homesickness. Like the letters you write, keep the conversation upbeat. Be sure and ask for a Visiting Day or care package wish list. If your child gets flustered and says she can't think of anything— reassure her that she can write you a letter with what she wants.

3. **No pressure** Don't use the telephone call to remind your child of your expectations about camp performance. If you have questions about your camper's progress in activities, such as how his tennis game is improving or whether he is meeting his swimming goals, ask the director, not your child.

Birthdays at a Distance

More than 50 years later, one mom can still remember celebrating her sixth birthday at camp! It was her first summer at sleepaway camp and when the special day arrived, "I was delighted because my mother had sent small gifts for each of the girls in the bunk and a slightly bigger present for me. We had a party in the bunk and my mother had arranged for a cake. I can still remember how special and important I felt. When I came home from camp, we celebrated again with a family birthday party."

Birthdays at camp are lots of fun. But talk to the director at your pre-camp interview to find out what is permitted from home—and what's not.

1. Will the camp provide a cake, or do you need to make arrangements at a local bakery? Can you send any food favorites from home?
2. Will it be a camp-wide celebration or just for your child's bunk?
3. Does the birthday camper get any special privileges on that day?
4. Can you speak to your child on her birthday? Or visit? (Even if visiting is permitted, you may decide that it will be more disruptive and difficult for your child if you do.)

When their child was to be at camp for her birthday, one mom scheduled a party *before* the end of school so that she could celebrate with her friends. Then on her actual birthday, her bunkmates decorated the cabin with handmade signs, presented her with impromptu gifts (candy from the canteen, funny "coupons" for hair braiding, and fortune telling), and the entire camp sang "happy birthday" to her at lunch.

VISITING DAY

As with most holidays, families are sometimes surprised, but shouldn't be, that emotions are rampant on Visiting Day at camp and run the full gamut of feelings, both good and bad. It can be an exciting day of reunion, but it can also prompt a return of homesickness (that has probably just abated); it can be an opportunity to show off the many skills acquired in just a few short weeks, but it can also be a time of disappointment if all does not go as planned. Especially for first-time campers and their parents, Visiting Day is an important milestone in the camp experience, and these tips will help make the day run more smoothly for all participants.

Plan Ahead

Hopefully, when you sent in your deposit for camp, you also put down a deposit for lodging for Visiting Day if you're going to need it. Local motels surrounding summer camps fill up fast. One Maryland family, whose son attended a camp in Maine, deliberately chose to stay in Portland, about an hour's ride from the camp. Since they were flying to Maine and would have to rent a car in any case, they didn't mind driving the extra time on Visiting Day. They discovered that the metropolitan room prices were no higher than those offered by the local motels around the camp (which boosted their rates significantly during Visiting Day weekend). Furthermore, their choice of accommodations was greater.

If You Live within Driving Distance

"Get up and get moving!" That's the advice of one veteran father for Visiting Day at his son's camp. The site was two hours from home and the gates opened at 9:30 A.M. When the family arrived at 9:40 it was clear that his son had grown anxious in just those few minutes.

Kids are on overdrive from the moment they get up in the morning of the Visiting Day. They can't wait to see you. Be there a few minutes early so when your child scans the crowds, he'll see a familiar face immediately.

What's Happening

Your child's camp will notify you about the Visiting Day program. Some camps permit parents to take their child off site, while others insist that the day is spent on the camp grounds. Again, you want to know what is "customary and usual" for the camp your child attends.

Many camps have the parents follow their child through a "typical" day, observing and interacting in the various programs. That means you might *watch* your child play in a softball game, take a swim lesson, work on a craft project. But then you might also choose to join your camper during free swim or play a game of tennis with him.

Visiting Day is an opportunity to discuss your child's progress with the counselor and activity specialist (although any serious problems should have been dealt with before Visiting Day). You're not looking for a straight-A report card, but rather an overview of how your youngster is enjoying this experience.

But that means you need to schedule some quiet one-on-one time with your camper before you leave. Take a walk around the campgrounds or seek out a quiet spot on the lawn and encourage your child to talk honestly and frankly about camp. Hopefully, what you will hear is that sometimes she misses you (understandable), but that in general she's having a lot of fun.

☼ Tell her that she might feel homesick briefly after Visiting Day—that's perfectly normal.

☼ Encourage her to share her feelings with the counselors and friends.

☼ Remind her how short a time it was until Visiting Day—and that it will be a similarly brief period before she is home.

But Suppose There Is a Problem?

But if your child complains about a counselor, bunkmate, or even continuing homesickness, you want to *empower* your camper to believe that she can handle the problem and find an acceptable solution.

☼ Listen carefully and respectfully to her complaint.

☼ Offer comfort and acceptance of any of the emotions she may feel.

☼ Provide a clear message that coming home is not the answer.

☼ Encourage her to believe that she can problem solve any issue, *and that it is a sign of maturity to ask for help.*

☼ Remind her that the camp staff is there to assist. Point out that even if the problem is with her own counselor, there are others on the staff whose job it is to listen and help.

If necessary, offer to accompany your child to discuss the problem with the camp director—*although if possible let the camper do the talking.* Follow up with a phone call, letter, or fax to the director when you go home.

Of course, if you believe that it's a serious problem that must be addressed immediately, or if you see an issue that troubles you, speak to the director before you leave. *Arrange a telephone appointment since it's unlikely that the director will have time during Visiting Day to give your problem the attention it deserves.*

Food, Glorious Food

Most camps permit you to bring food into camp on Visiting Day, but many insist that the food be consumed that day and any leftovers removed from the bunk. One counselor recalls the "banquet" of goodies that her charges enjoyed after all the parents went home. But then the camp donated the remaining goodies to a homeless shelter.

Ask about the camp's policy on food. If it's a camp affiliated with a religion, ask if there are any prohibitions on food brought into the camp. Some programs that keep strictly kosher do not want any food, even packaged food marked kosher, brought into the camp.

MEDICAL ISSUES

The medical problems at camp are usually mild and easily treatable. The staff has to be prepared in case of an emergency, but most visits to the infirmary require little or no treatment. As one camp doctor remarked: "Remember that many of the campers' minor maladies are just a bad case of homesickness." Experienced camp medical staff are accustomed to helping children cope with the blues. One mother got a call from the camp infirmary when her son checked in with unspecified complaints. They kept him overnight, and he slept for 10 hours straight. The camper later admitted that mostly he was just tired and needed some sleep.

An article in *Clinical Pediatrics,* a medical journal, analyzed a typical pediatric practice at a summer sleepaway camp. There were 694 campers (between the ages of 9 and 16), and 266 adult staff members. There were a total of 895 visits to the infirmary during the four-week period studied, but 190 children were evaluated on more than one occasion. The basic complaints were sports injuries (lacerations, abrasions, splinters, bruises, blisters, and sprains) and upper respiratory ailments (stuffed nose, sore throat, cough, congestion, and conjunctivitis). The authors concluded that "aside from an increase in minor sports-related injuries, the health problems of children in camp are not significantly different in type or severity from those they experience at home. Furthermore, children attending camp can be relied upon to accurately report their complaints and receive appropriate medical attention." The authors added an interesting conclusion, ". . . in view of the benign nature of most of the visits, it is likely that children overutilize the infirmary and seek attention for problems that might otherwise be dismissed at home."

The authors also noted that "younger-age and female campers were more likely to visit the infirmary." *Remind your son that it is a sign of maturity to seek help when needed. There is no need for any "macho" behavior if he is hurt.*

If the camp calls to tell you that your child is sick, you want to know what's wrong, what's being done, and under what circumstances a specialist will be called. Don't hesitate to call back, frequently if necessary, to check on your child's progress.

It may be difficult for both your child and you to deal with an unfamiliar health professional. Remember that one of the reasons you selected this camp is that you trusted (and checked) the director to hire a good staff. This extends to the medical professionals on the staff as well. Still as one doctor recalls: "one set of parents wouldn't even let me treat their son who had some mild wheezing but preferred to drive three hours to their regular doctor and then back three hours to camp." This is not necessarily a good message to give to your child. You want him to develop confidence in his own ability to judge the severity of the problem, as well as to be able to seek and get help from competent medical professionals. If you don't trust the medical staff at the camp, perhaps it isn't the right camp for your child.

If your child breaks a bone during camp, you may ask that the X rays be sent to your own doctor or orthopedist, even while your child is treated on site. If your doctor has any questions, he can consult with the specialist near the camp or you could always bring the child home. Many families have brought their injured youngsters home for treatment and then sent the child back to complete the camp season. As one 13-year-old camper explained: "Even with a broken arm, camp was more fun than being home!"

COMING HOME

When the camp season is over, the same child who shed tears for leaving home may now cry over leaving camp. Hopefully, it's been a wonderful experience and she has made new friends.

The reentry home can be hectic, but here are several practical tips to make it easier.

1. **Check for lice** Yucky, but necessary. One mother remembers her daughter standing on the doorstep, bags in hand, saying her hair was itchy. "I immediately checked and unfortunately the little critters were there. She got in the shower while I took her clothes directly to the washing machine. Otherwise, I would have had to go through the whole process of changing sheets, vacuuming rugs, and risking infec-

tion of the rest of the family." Lice are an unfortunate possibility when kids are in close quarters. Save yourself heartache—check!

2. **Sort and toss** Go through the camp clothes, discarding those that are beyond hope. Save yourself washing an article of clothing that is irreparable or badly stained.

3. **Did the tennis racquet come home?** Check the packing list to make sure that all important items returned from camp. If not, call and ask the camp to check for lost items.

4. **Store in a safe place** Store together the trunk and equipment that your child needs for camp. Write notes to remind yourself about what was needed—and what wasn't—and store with camp equipment.

Your child will undoubtedly be tired, probably in need of a bath, excited, missing her camp friends, eager to see her home friends, and hungry (you can take care of the latter easily). While you want to talk about the camp experience, remember that it's all a jumble in the beginning.

☼ Give your child some space and time to sort through the experience and then talk about it.

☼ Avoid, if possible, leaving immediately for vacation. Your youngster needs to spend at least a day or two at home.

☼ Encourage her to keep in touch with camp friends. It makes it easier to return to camp the following year. It also teaches your child about the value of friendship and the steps necessary to maintain a long-distance relationship. If the camp sponsors a midwinter reunion, arrange for your child to attend.

☼ Encourage your child to make a scrapbook of the camp experience. Include any photos, awards, drawings, journal entries, etc. It's a great way to preserve the camp memories.

Planning Ahead to the Next Season

Parents are sometimes surprised that around January their once eager, now veteran camper begins to question a return to overnight camp the following summer. Even if the experience was absolutely terrific, the camper may also remember the homesickness and brief periods of unhappiness.

Reassure your child that this is typical. Take out the camp scrapbook she created, and talk about the fun and funny times she had at camp. Acknowledge that homesickness can reoccur, but that it passes much more quickly the second summer.

Sleepaway camp offers children a unique opportunity for independence and growth. Children who suffer from chronic illness or disabilities can also enjoy the sleepaway camp experience. In the next chapter, you'll find information on how to evaluate special needs camps. You'll also learn about specialty camps. If your child wants to focus on a specific field of study or sport, there's a camp just for him.

Chapter **6**

SPECIALTY CAMPS:
A UNIQUE KIND OF FUN

One 11-year-old baseball fanatic spent a dream week pursuing his favorite game at a sports camp held on a college campus. The campers lived in the air-conditioned college dorms, which had private baths for each room. Sugar cereals and soda were available at every meal. Baseball in one form or another took up about 14 hours a day. Any free time was spent playing video games, ordering in pizza, watching slasher movies, or just hanging out. On the way home from baseball camp, the family stopped to visit a traditional overnight camp. Looking at the bunks, tents, shower facilities, etc., the 11-year-old turned and puzzled asked, "Why would anyone want to live like this for the summer?"

Looking for a special camp that focuses almost exclusively on an interest or sport that captures your child's attention? Music, computer, art, entrepreneurship, photography, chess—there's a summer program that explores each of these areas and many others in depth. Enthusiasts of any sport can find a specialty camp to fill their day. In fact, some sports camps have very narrow specialties, for example, a basketball camp exclusively for point guards; a soccer camp just for goalies.

And summer camp fun is available to all children, even those who suffer from chronic illness, life-threatening disease, physical, emotional, or learning disabilities. For these children, camp is more than fun. They help a youngster adjust to the disease/disability, build a peer support network, and develop self-confidence and coping skills.

In this chapter, you'll find the information you need to judge the safety and strength of these specialized camps.

SPORTS CAMPS FOR THE ENTHUSIAST

Why a sports camp?

☼ If your child wants to improve his skills, then a sports camp may be just the answer. You can find day camp and residential programs for almost any sport you name.

☼ For the child who hopes to make the select travel team or move up to the varsity level at school, enrolling in a sports camp may just tip the balance in her favor.

☼ For the exceptional athlete, sports camps are good for networking. College coaches often scout for talent at these programs, and in fact, many college coaches run their own sports camps. One high school soccer player was tempted to skip a summer soccer camp, but his coach warned that it was important for possible college recruitment that he attend at least one of the summer programs.

☼ And even for nonathletes, who enjoy the game but aren't particularly gifted, a sports camp may still be a fun place to be, surrounded by similar enthusiasts.

What a Sports Camp Is and Isn't

Before enrolling your child in any sports camp, both of you need to understand the limited focus of these programs. Whether your camper is a baseball nut, soccer enthusiast, fencer, sailor, hockey player, swimmer, diver, scuba diver, runner, basketball player, football star—whatever the sport, the day is built around playing it!

Any free time is limited. It's generally strictly up to the camper whether he takes advantage of any of the other facilities, for example, a pool or basketball court, that are located on the campsite.

HIT THE SHOWERS

Hygiene is a personal responsibility at many of these special camps. Is your child ready for the responsibility? One mother found the answer when she went to pick up her 10-year-old after a week at baseball camp. Alarmed at the strong aroma emanating from her son, she asked, "Haven't you showered at all this week?" Indignantly, the son replied, "Of course, on Tuesday." The mother asked, "Did you brush your teeth?" Even more indignantly, the son answered, "Of course, when I showered."

SPORTS CAMP SCHEDULE

7:30	Wake up and breakfast
8:30	Warm ups
9:30–11:30	First session including skills instruction and practice
12:00	Lunch
1:00–3:00	Second session including skills instruction and practice
3:00–4:30	Free Time
4:30–6:00	Third Session, games
6:30	Dinner
7:30–9:00	Classroom instruction and strategy sessions
10:00	Curfew

Friendships are secondary to the sport. As one camper pointed out: "You hang out with other campers at night, but it's not like a regular camp where making new friends is part of the whole idea of camp."

And supervision is different—and some might suggest less intense. Often these programs are held in rented facilities at local schools or colleges. Campers may stay in dormitories and may or may not share a room. It's not the same as living in a bunk with eight other kids. This is not a program designed to help a camper who is suffering from homesickness. Counselors will be sympathetic, but a certain level of maturity is expected of participants. Campers are largely responsible for their level of participation. They are expected to get themselves to practice on time; report injuries; choose their own meal selections from a cafeteria-style dining hall; go to sleep when it's curfew; make a decision whether to participate or not in free time activities; be responsible for their own hygiene, laundry, and communications with home.

Finally, the level of competition at these camps can be intense. The directors and counselors may be varsity coaches, college varsity players, or play on professional teams. They may have high expectations for participants. At the same time, the campers may also have the skills to expect a high level of play. You need to know that your child wants to be in that environment and can handle the pressure.

How to Find the Right Sports Camp

There are several ways to find a sports camp.

* ✷ Word of mouth.
* ✷ Flyers or brochures on community, school, or college bulletin boards.
* ✷ The Internet. Many sports camps maintain web sites.
* ✷ Varsity coaches at the high school and college level may either run a program or know one they recommend to their players.
* ✷ Sports magazines often carry advertisements for these kinds of camps.
* ✷ Camp guides (see Appendix 5).

What to Ask the Director?

Many sports camps are well established and have been in business for many years. But unlike traditional overnight camps, the questions you need to ask are more specific.

1. How long has the camp been in operation? How long at this particular location?

2. If the director has a "big" name, for example, a professional ball player, how involved is he in the program? Often these sports celebrities lend their name to a camp, but their involvement is limited to visits and autographs.

3. Who are the coaches? What is their training? Preferably you are looking for varsity college coaches with college players as assistants. How much of the staff is returning from the previous year?

4. What is the ratio of instructors to campers? How are the groups organized? By age? By skill level? By weight? Is there room for movement to a higher skill level once the camp begins?

5. How many campers are returning from the previous year?

6. Does the camp run a complete evaluation of skills at the beginning of camp and then a second one at the end to judge progress? Will the camp provide a written evaluation of the camper at the end of the program?

7. What are the ages of the campers who attend? If your child is 10 years old and the majority of the players are in their teens, it may not be an appropriate program, even if the camp does accept players that young. Ask for the number of campers enrolled in your child's age group.

8. What is the level of play? Some camps accept players at all skill levels; others require a tryout and the player must be a "select" or "elite" player. How is the skill level determined? How many campers are enrolled at that level?

REFERENCE CHECKS

If you don't know any other families who have used this particular sports camp, ask the director for references. You'll want to know:

☼ What did the camper like about the program?
☼ What did the camper dislike about the program?
☼ What did the parents think of the supervision?
☼ Did the camper's skills noticeably improve?

SESSION LENGTH

Most sports camps programs are built around a five- or six-day schedule. Campers enroll by the week, with most attending no more than two weeks in the season. Some campers choose to attend several sports camps, sometimes in the same sport, in the same summer. They learn from the different experts and drills in each program.

How Much Does It Cost?

Residential sports camps cost between $400 and $800 per week. Sports day camps begin around $200 per week.

Be sure and ask if there are any additional costs: equipment? uniforms? videotaping? private lessons?

OTHER SPECIAL INTERESTS CAMPS

Name the interest, and it's a sure bet that there is an accompanying summer program. There are loads of camps for youngsters interested in music, computers, and nature study. In addition, there are programs for gifted and talented students; archaeology programs; history programs; science programs; rocketry camps—to list all the possibilities is nearly impossible.

The value of these camps, like a sports camp, is to reinforce and encourage a child's interests and abilities in a particular subject. These camps have the luxury of time. Campers can focus on a single subject without other demands or distractions. And like sports camps, a gifted child may attract college interest by attending one of these special interest camps.

Some special interest camps are more serious about pursuing the special interest than others. You know your child and how much time he wants to devote to a particular subject. A serious musician may not want or need a sports component to the camp program. Other campers may want to continue their music studies in the summer, but also want the bonfires and sports component of a regular summer camp program. You can find camps to meet the interests of both kinds of musicians.

But finding a program and checking it out is basically the same process whatever the interest.

The key points remain the same: *You want a safe, secure environment in which your child can pursue his special interests.*

To find a program to match your child's interest and level of expertise, use all the same techniques you would if you were searching for a sports camp or traditional camp: word of mouth; flyers or brochures on community, school, or college bulletin boards; the Internet; teachers at the high school and college level; specialty magazines; and camp guides (see Appendix 5). Your child's teacher is an especially good resource. Their professional magazines and journals often carry listings and descriptions of appropriate summer programs.

CHECK IT OUT

Many of the questions you want to ask directors of special interest camps are the same as those discussed earlier (see chapter 3). Essentially you want to know: What will my child study; who will teach him; what equipment will he use; how will you evaluate his progress?

For example, if your child is interested in attending a music camp, you would ask:

☼ Who makes up the staff of the camp? What are their credentials? If you are not familiar with the subject area, your child's music teacher can review and judge the staff credentials.

☼ Where do the majority of campers come from? Is it a local, regional, national, or even international program? Do many campers return year after year? The makeup of the camper population will probably influence the level of play. The larger, more established music camp programs draw excellent student musicians from around the world.

☼ Do the campers have group lessons, private lessons, or both? (Is there an additional charge for private lessons?)

☼ Do the campers perform in large and small group ensembles? How often do they perform? Who makes up the audience?

☼ How specialized is the music program? Some camps concentrate on a particular style (jazz, classical, chamber music), where others offer a broad range of music study.

☼ Does the camp require an audition to gain entrance? This may make it more difficult to attend the camp, but elevate the level of play.

☼ Who provides the instruments and who maintains them at camp?

☼ Are there any evaluations of the campers?

Similar questions could be asked of directors of any special interest camp, but tailored to that particular subject. For example, at a computer camp, you would want to know what equipment the campers use; what software; how much time is spent on original programming; who are the teachers.

Suppose My Child's the Expert, Not Me?

Don't worry if you are not familiar with a particular subject and don't think you can adequately judge the quality of the program. You can ask others to help you assess the level of the program, while you still check out the safety and security of the camp.

☼ You can ask local experts or teachers to review a camp program or curriculum.

☼ You can post a question on an Internet bulletin board or news group.

☼ You can ask at the high school or local college for help in assessing a program.

SPECIAL NEEDS CAMPS

If your child has a special need, if she is physically, emotionally, or learning disabled, you may want to consider a camp that specializes in these issues. There are many advantages, for both the camper and her family, to participating in a program specifically designed for children who share a common disability.

ADVANTAGES OF A SPECIAL NEEDS CAMP

There are camps for almost every disability. Although many mainstream camps can accommodate children with disabilities, you may still decide that a specialized camp will benefit both you and your child.

Medically Safe Environment If your child has a chronic or life-threatening disease, there is the security of knowing that your youngster is surrounded by professionals who are trained to treat this specific disease. For parents whose child has been recently diagnosed with a disease, a specialized camp offers a good, *safe*, summer experience for their child, when they (the parents) are feeling especially vulnerable. But even children who have had their condition for years can still benefit from being in a medically safe environment where they can take risks knowing that there is a strong safety net.

Peer Support Group One of the most important benefits of a special needs camp is it provides a child with a *peer* support group. At one of these programs, the child finds himself surrounded by children his age who have the same disease/disability as he has. This can be especially helpful for adolescents who can connect with other teens who must cope with many of the same issues, for example, the coach who doesn't want a special needs student on the team.

Empathy As the mother of a learning disabled child remarked: "At camp, my daughter discovered that lots of children have the same problems in school that she has—and frankly some have more serious difficulties. She learned empathy."

Just One of the Gang "A child who has diabetes may be the only one in his school with the disease," says the executive director of an overnight camp for children with diabetes, "but at camp, diabetes is a given. In some ways, the campers don't have to think about it anymore. Everyone has diabetes, all the campers, and most of the staff." That can be an important psychological relief for a child with a disability or disease.

Camp Does the Adapting, Not the Camper At a special needs camp, diet, activities, equipment, physical layout, etc., have all been developed or adapted to meet the specific needs of the campers. The camper doesn't have to make the adjustments to meet the demands of a mainstream camp.

Coping Skills/Education Some camps have a formal educational component to their program where children are taught to deal medically with their disease. In other programs the educational component is more informal, but not necessarily less effective. "It's not unusual for a child to give herself her first insulin shot at camp," explains the diabetes camp director, even if there is no formal educational component to the camp program. "The campers learn through interaction with one another. It's not unusual for campers who have never given themselves insulin injections, to give themselves their first shot at camp (under supervision) because they see other kids do it."

Family Respite Even under the best of circumstances, a child with a chronic disease or disability changes the family dynamics. There may be added stresses and responsibilities, which affect siblings. Enrolling a child with special needs in a medically safe summer environment may give parents and siblings a respite from the daily responsibility or demands that the disease places on the family.

Role Models "The campers see counselors and staff members who are leading full, complete lives with the disease; they see people pursuing their dreams, unstopped by the illness." This powerful message is a long-term benefit of these camps.

Fun Probably the most important ingredient of any summer camp experience *for any child* is fun. It's critical that whatever else the summer camp program does for your special needs child, it provides a schedule based on the concept that these are still kids.

An Educated Staff At these camps, the entire staff, nurses, counselors, dieticians, specialists, have all been trained in dealing with the disease/disability. This staff understands not only the physical implications of the disease/disability, but the psychological effects as well.

No Break in Therapy Depending on the structure of the program, campers can continue with therapy or tutoring. This can be essential for many experts believe that taking a summer vacation from therapy can undermine the progress of the previous months. And for children with learning disabilities, it can make the transition back to school much easier if they have continued to work during the summer. One mother says that the summer her daughter spent at a camp for children with learning disabilities made the critical difference in her successful transfer from a learning disabilities school to a mainstream school. The camp reinforced the necessary study skills, as well as worked with her daughter on her summer reading assignments.

STARTING THE SEARCH

To find the right camp for your child begin with your doctor. Specialists are often on the advisory boards or medical consultants to these types of camps. Health care professionals understand the value of a summer camp experience for all kids—regardless of disability or disease. Word of mouth from parents whose children share the same disability is also an excellent resource.

Other good sources of information are: parent support groups; camp fairs organized for families with special needs; teachers/guidance counselors; camp advisers; on-line web sites and targeted news groups; *Guide to Accredited Camps*, published by the ACA; and national/local support organizations.

CHECK IT OUT

Once you have a list of possible camps, the steps you follow to check out the program are similar to those of any parents considering a summer camp program (see chapter 3). If possible, visit the camp while it's in session; interview the director; and check references with other parents whose children have attended the camp.

But before you enroll your child, you need to know:

1. How the camp program, facilities, dietary plan are adapted to meet the special needs of the campers.

A COORDINATED EFFORT

Work closely with your child's doctor, therapist, and teacher to ensure that the summer camp activities will reinforce, if not strengthen her daily life. Other important steps:

☼ Ask your health care professional and, where necessary, your child's current teacher, to provide the camp with a current evaluation of your youngster's condition. This will help in planning for the summer.

☼ Give the camp permission to discuss any problems or ask questions of any health care professional with whom your child is working.

☼ Discuss with your doctor if any medication needs to be changed to meet the demands of the more physically challenging program of a summer camp.

☼ Ask that the medical director/staff provides you with a written evaluation of your child's progress at the end of camp. You will want to give it to the professionals who work with your child during the school year.

2. How the educational component, if there is one, is integrated into the camp day. One camper who attended a program for children with learning disabilities was disgruntled over the amount of "work" she had to do at camp. Classes were held from 9 to 12 every day, with more traditional camp activities scheduled in the afternoon and evening. This 12-year-old felt there wasn't enough of a balance to the program—although the academic progress she made that summer was exceptional.

3. The range of disabilities in the camp. Some camps are more targeted than others. One family enrolled their above-average-intelligence son who has spina bifida into a county-sponsored camp for children with special needs. But the range of disabilities was too great. He was grouped with children who had both physical and mental disabilities. While the experience taught him that many children were more severely disabled than he, it was not a successful summer camp experience.

MAINSTREAMING YOUR CHILD

Depending on the severity of your child's disability, you may decide that a mainstream camp is the right place for your child. This is a decision that must be a collaborative effort made in consultation with the camp, your child's doctors, perhaps an educational psychologist, and *drawing upon your own parental sense of who your child is and what is best for him.*

Many mainstream camps are prepared to adapt the camp experience to the special needs of a child. For example, a deaf child attended a mainstream overnight camp for several years. There were a few adjustments necessary, but none required extraordinary effort. For example, when teaching a swim lesson, the instructor had to make sure that the camper was facing him so the child could read the teacher's lips. On the other hand, some of the safety rules already in place made the adaptation easy. The deaf child's "swim buddy" was responsible for alerting the camper that the whistle had been blown when the session was over.

Mainstream camps often have to adapt their program to meet the needs of individual children who are not classified as "special needs." For example, it's not unusual for a child to attend camp with a broken leg—not ideal, of course, but hardly unusual. So adaptations are frequently made.

The advantages of enrolling your child in a mainstream program are:

Expectations The expectations for your child may be more demanding and children attempt to meet the level of expectation. For example, in a mainstream camp where speech is the appropriate method of communication, a child with a lag in speech development may be more likely to use language to communicate.

Acceptance Merely being in a regular environment may ease acceptance of a child with a disability. Peers, parents, and the community will see that a disabled child can function in a regular program. As educators have learned, having a child with special needs in the class is helpful for the development of *all* children. Children learn that disabilities need not affect friendship or an individual's abilities to function in a community.

Social Cues Children with disabilities may learn to interact more easily with mainstream children if they are living and playing with them on a normal basis. It may also help some disabled youngsters learn the social cues necessary for mainstream interaction.

Already Mainstreamed Many children with disabilities or chronic diseases are already mainstreamed in school and have learned how to adapt their situation to the mainstream. Camp is just a continuation of their regular existence.

But some experts see disadvantages in mainstreaming a special needs child:

☼ For the more medically fragile child, the camp environment and staff, while well intentioned, may not have the expertise or equipment to cope with the demands of this type of camper.

☼ It may be more difficult to coordinate treatment schedules. An intensive therapy program may be too demanding in terms of hours needed or because of the physical demands it puts on the child.

☼ A specialized camp program may offer a community of support for both the child and her family, which may not be available from a mainstream program.

☼ Peer pressure may not be supportive. The child with spina bifida, who had been mainstreamed since kindergarten in a regular classroom, found that healthy kids were sometimes angry or disgruntled when the pace of a game had to be slowed in order to accommodate his participation. For example, when the group played softball, while he could bat from a wheelchair, another camper had to run the bases for him. It may not be nice, but some campers began to voice their resentment, making the disabled child feel uncomfortable.

☼ Inadequate staff training can be disastrous. Even if a camp attempts to provide a strong staff training program, it may not be enough to deal with your child's disability. Just understanding the physical manifestations of the disease, may not be enough for a young counselor to understand the wider ramifications of a disease or disability.

Working with the Mainstream Camp

It's critically important, if you choose a mainstream camp for your child, that you establish a strong communication link between you and the camp staff. *You must be honest and open about your child's personality and needs.*

Some families worry that if they are too blunt about the effects of the disability or their child's personality, the camp director will not accept their child into the program. But this is a certain recipe for disaster—and this would be true for *any* child.

The more a director knows, the better prepared he can be and the more training he can provide his staff. Furthermore, if a director has seri-

---

IS IT FUN, YET?

Families whose children have disabilities are constantly worried about the pressures or problems their children will endure from peers. It's not easy and each family has to decide how far and how often they will demand inclusion. *You know your child best.* You may decide that in the long run, your child will benefit from inclusion in all activities, even if it requires your child to face some peer opposition. Other parents want the summer to be "easier" with the thought there are enough battles to fight during the school year.

Include your child in the decision-making process. What does he want to do? Is he making the decision based on fear or a cool assessment of the situation? Does he understand all the pros and cons of each situation? Is he willing to work to make the summer a success?

---

ous doubts whether the camp is appropriate for your youngster, you need to know that up front and make other arrangements.

Again, give the camp director permission to ask questions of your child's doctor, therapist, or teacher. And it's important that you have a director who isn't afraid to ask questions—you don't expect him to be an expert in your child's disability or illness.

THE BEST OF BOTH WORLDS

Some parents combine a mainstream camp experience with a few weeks at a special needs camp. It may offer your child the best of both worlds—integrating her in the mainstream community, while providing all the advantages of a special needs camp. There are, of course, scheduling and budget considerations, but this may be a good solution, depending on your child's current condition.

Special interest and special needs camps expand the summer camp options. As your child enters adolescence, his needs may change and you'll want even more choices. In the next chapter, you'll find an array of possibilities for your teenager—including staying home and getting a job!

Chapter 7

TEEN TOURS AND MORE:
THE FUN CONTINUES IN ADOLESCENCE

There was a part of me that wondered if it was just too indulgent to send my daughter on a teen trip to the Pacific Northwest. I wondered if she could handle not only the physical challenges, but also the emotional demands of living with 10 other teens, none of whom she knew. But I believe it was money well spent. She came back brimming with self-confidence because she had handled the difficult hiking and camping demands of this incredible journey. But even more important, I could sense a new level of maturity in her. Learning to live with other teens, being responsible for herself and as part of the group, taught her a lot about herself. It was a good preparation for going to college—and it had nothing to do with academics.

Some parents joke that the most important qualification for a teen summer program is that it begins the first day of vacation and ends the day before school begins. Living with an adolescent is often like living in the Twilight Zone. Sometimes it seems as if you are on one planet, and your teenager is in another galaxy. Language and customs of teens are different from ordinary, parent-type mortals.

But while choosing the right summer activity for a teen may be more complicated than selecting a general interest camp for a younger child, the rewards can be even richer. A teenager is in the midst of an incredible growth spurt. There is the literal physical change you may see when your teen arrives home from an eight-week camp stay two inches taller. But equally important are the emotional, spiritual, intellectual, social changes that a challenging summer program can produce in a teenager. As he is "stretched" and encouraged to try something new, as he expands his horizons, he sees the world—his peers—*himself* in a new light.

Although finding the right summer program for teens is different than finding a good camp for a nine-year-old, some of the basics are the same: you still want a safe, secure, *appropriate* environment. But teenagers need—and are ready for—not only new challenges, but greater independence. You will also find that as your child gets older, instead of looking at camps that might be good for several years, you are more interested in programs that meet your child's needs for one summer only. You will need to reexamine your choice each year as your child matures and his interests expand.

WHEN TO START

If you're living with a teenager, you already know that they are part kid, part adult. You often don't know which "person" you're going to meet when you come to the breakfast table! Planning a summer program in November makes sense for a nine-year-old, but may be more difficult with an adolescent because her interests and emotions are going through such enormous changes. But because many good programs fill up quickly, you still need to focus early so that your child has the widest range of choices.

Younger vs. Older Teens

It's important to keep in mind when choosing a program that the needs, interests, and abilities of a 13-year-old are quite different from the 16- or 17-year-old high schooler. Furthermore, when considering programs, keep in mind not only your child's chronological age, but his *maturity* as well. Parents often express concern about the level of supervision in many of the programs designed for teens.

While teen programs impose curfews, campers have greater independence of movement during the day. You need to determine if your youngster is ready for that kind of freedom. One mother explains her rationale behind choosing different baseball camps for her two sons. "We sent our older boy to baseball camp when he was 13. The camp had a great reputation, but the supervision was somewhat lax. But my older son was so mature and responsible that I knew he could handle the freedom. On the other hand, I absolutely knew it was the wrong place for my younger son. At the same age, he didn't have the judgment to exercise self-control in a looser environment."

"LET'S TALK"

There are lots of summer choices for teens, and the best way to start is to sit down and talk with your adolescent. In fact, searching for a meaningful summer program is a good way to strengthen the parent-teen relationship. It's an opportunity to discuss interests, concerns, values. While a private camp adviser (see chapter 2) may be very helpful in directing you to specific programs, you and your teen need to talk first about what each of you wants the summer to be.

But before you begin, first, make it clear that you really want to hear *his* answer, not the response *he thinks* you want to hear. You're trying to establish a dialogue and that depends on honesty and respect from both parties. Listen carefully to what your teen is telling you. His views and yours may not be as irreconcilable as they may appear at first glance. And when you model good, respectful behavior for his views, it's more likely that he will respond in kind.

The obvious place to begin is the simple question: *What do you want to do this summer?* Write down his goals for the summer on a piece of paper, with your goals opposite it so you can mix and match your responses.

Of course, his first response may be "nothing." Other possibilities are:

- ☼ do something exciting
- ☼ be with my friends
- ☼ hang out at the mall
- ☼ get a good tan
- ☼ I don't know

But even if "getting a good tan" (with sunblock, of course) is the goal, you may be able to find a program or activity that meets his needs *and* yours.

A PLACE IN TIME

Encourage your teen to keep a journal of his summer activities. Whether he has a job, studies, volunteers, takes a trip, or any combination, this is an important time in your child's life. The thoughts and emotions of the moment are important. He will have the journal not only as a record of what happened, but as a place to review and reflect on those same events and issues months, even years, later. It will give him a unique perspective on that time in his life.

But since this is a two-way conversation, you need to list what you want your teen to accomplish this summer. You may feel that your teen needs:

* ☼ exercise
* ☼ to explore his interests on a more challenging plane
* ☼ to study on a college level
* ☼ to see the world/country/region
* ☼ to volunteer to help someone/somewhere
* ☼ to earn some money
* ☼ SAT preparation
* ☼ to relax after a stressful academic year

A PATCHWORK PROGRAM

One of the best ways to reconcile your goals with your child's is to piece together the summer with activities from both your lists. Although it is more difficult and the logistics may be more time consuming than if you could find a single program that fills the summer, combining a series of activities through the summer may make the time well spent.

By participating in different programs or activities during the summer, your teen also gets a broader experience. For example, one 16-year-old had her heart set on returning to the theater arts camp she had attended the previous two summers; her parents believed it was time for her to have a real work experience in an office setting. The compromise? The teen attended one, three-week session at camp, then spent the next five weeks working in an insurance office.

I DON'T WANT TO LEAVE HOME

One of the major issues may be whether or not your teen wants to be home for the summer. Even if he has been a veteran sleepaway camper for several years, he may decide that this summer he wants to hang out at home. While he may actually enjoy your company, it's more likely that he wants to be around his friends.

In fact, you need to be realistic about whether or not his friends will be at home during the summer. If he is basing his plans on assumptions or conversations over the lunch table, he may discover that when June rolls around he is the only one of his group still around. *Double-check what his friends will be doing during the vacation before you make a final decision.*

You need to explore his reasons for wanting to stay home, and how it will impact his—and your—summer plans. Of course, the primary question is: *What will he do if stays home?* If there are programs, jobs, volunteer opportunities that can usefully occupy his time, this may be a reasonable option. But you also need to consider how his decision will impact your family life.

* If he drives, will he need access to a car to get to his summer activity?
* If he doesn't drive, will he need a parent to provide transportation?
* If the job/volunteer activity/program is not full time, will he need additional supervision if there are no adults at home during the day?
* What will he do *and with whom* when he is not engaged in the summer activity?

TIME FOR FAMILY

Teenagers are the first ones to beg out of family outings, vacations, even meals. They're often embarrassed to be seen with you, bored with the activities, worried that they will look "lame" if caught with parents and younger siblings.

But for their sake—and yours—build in family time when planning the summer activities. It's important to maintain the family ties and communication.

STAY-AT-HOME SUMMER

If you decide that your teen will choose a local summer program, then it's important to establish summertime rules, expectations, chores, and schedules. This is especially important if this is the first summer in several years that your youngster has been at home. As one mother wailed when confronted with her teen son's decision to take a local camp job: "I love my son, but I treasure those eight weeks when both kids are away at camp and it's just my husband and myself. We eat out, take day trips, see a movie whenever we want . . . now what am I going to do?"

SETTING SUMMER RULES

Parenting a teen is often a judgment call—yours and his. Some families have very strict rules, others a more laissez-faire approach. Most of us know both kinds of families and frankly have seen success stories—and obvious failures—using both parenting styles. You need to do what feels right for you and your child. It's not that you need to suddenly make up rules if you haven't had them in your family. *On the other hand, you'll want to think through what you expect and lay out the ground rules so that the summer isn't a big surprise for either you or your teen.* Consider the following areas of possible conflict and decide how you want to handle these issues.

CURFEW

Now that school is out, what is a reasonable time for your teen to be at home? Although you probably have given up on a bedtime, you do want to know where he is and with whom. Furthermore, you want to know he's in the house at a certain time. While his summer program may not require him to be up as early as school days, you will still probably want to establish a curfew that works for everyone in the family. Even if he doesn't have to be up in the morning, you probably do! Furthermore, a curfew often is a convenient excuse for a teen to leave a social situation. *"Sorry, I have to be in by 11:30."* Blame it on Mom.

One family mounted a blackboard in the kitchen so the children (there were 10 of them) could leave messages about where they were going, with whom, and when they would be home. If a youngster didn't plan to be home for a meal, a message or call was expected. But as this experienced mother pointed out, "I think much of this is *common courtesy*. I leave those kinds of messages for my husband!"

CHORES

Summertime and the livin' is easy? But if your teen is going to be around the house some or all of the day, count on higher food bills and more dishes in the sink. You need to make clear your expectations about cleanup and chores.

Do you expect your teen to assume more household responsibility during the summer months than she does during the school year? One family, who had hired a neighborhood teen to mow the lawn during the summers while their child had been at camp, now required their own teen to assume responsibility for lawn care since he would be home.

What about baby-sitting younger siblings (see page 146 for teen summer jobs)? Pay or no pay? Work out the parameters of the employer-employee relationship with your teen *before* the job starts. One mother paid her two teens for baby-sitting help sometimes (usually on Saturday nights), but also assumed that there were other times when watching the younger sibling was just another household chore. "It seemed unfair that I was depriving my kids of an opportunity to make some money since they were getting calls from other families in search of a baby-sitter. So I decided that I would pay for baby-sitting on Saturday night, but not during the week."

FRIENDS

One of the attractions about staying at home is the opportunity to be with friends. But do you want to have any rules about how many friends, if any, can be in the house if there are no adults home? Some parents are comfortable and permit their teens to have friends over with or without adult supervision. Others set limits; still others insist that no friends of the opposite sex can be in the house without adults present, even if the teens are not involved romantically.

Base your decision on your own values and judgment about your child and the friends involved. As one mother explains: "I really trust that my daughter who's 16 will use good judgment when she has friends over, whether I'm there or not, so I don't limit the number or frequency. On the other hand, I do restrict the number of friends my 14-year-old son can have over because they're still at the roughhousing stage and I'm worried that things will get out of hand if I'm not home." Another parent expressed similar concerns and added: "I also worry that if there are too many kids over when I'm not there it will be too much noise for my neighbors."

One mother expressed concern about a specific friend of her teen son. "I'm more wary of having this one kid over, even if I am home, so I've told my son this friend can't come over when my husband or I aren't home. But there are other friends of my son's that I wouldn't give it a second thought." Again, if you establish the ground rules in the beginning, you may be able to avoid some problems.

COED VISITS?

Some parents are very relaxed about it, others have stricter rules. "I told my daughter it just doesn't look right if she has boys over when there isn't an adult home. I'm concerned about her reputation even though I do respect her judgment." Another father was more philosophical, "I trust my son's judgment, and frankly I trust his girlfriend's judgment even more!" Other families suggest it depends on how much time and how often the situation will arise. "I worried the summer my daughter was 15. She had her first boyfriend and I didn't want them to be spending hours together alone in the house while I was at work. It was one of the reasons I insisted that she get a job at the local day camp. I wanted her to have a structure to the day and not just endless time to spend with her boyfriend." This is an opportunity to think and talk about how you want to handle a situation that may come up more frequently as your kids get older.

CLEANUP

One mother set household rules for her four teens who were home during the summer. Although each had a summer job or program that occupied them during the day, they still got home before her and her husband in the evening. "After a few days of finding a sink full of dishes when I walked in the door, I insisted that the kitchen had to be cleaned up before I started dinner. Since they were also eating me out of house and home, I finally set the rule that I would buy sodas and snacks once a week and if we ran out, then it was up to them to go to the supermarket and buy them with their own money." Again, figure out what works for your family. The plus side of setting some basic rules is that it teaches kids responsibility—which is a life lesson in itself.

TRANSPORTATION

One 14-year-old found a great internship at a science museum. It was unfortunately 20 miles from his home, with no easy access by public transportation. If getting to and from the summer program is going to be a problem for your teen, it's time to get creative. In this teen's case, the program was structured so that the interns were scheduled to work either two mornings or two afternoons a week. Instead, the administration was willing to be flexible and permitted the nonresident teen to work one full day a week. The father then arranged to go to work an hour late and leave an hour early one day a week so his son could participate in the program. It was a unique opportunity, but demanded flexibility on the part of *all* the adults—the program staff and the parents.

Other possibilities besides public transportation include paying a local teen to provide car service; car pools; taxis; and a novel idea—walking, biking, Rollerblading! One teen couldn't believe it when his mother was unruffled at the idea of him walking two miles each morning to a music camp at the local elementary school.

Don't let the lack of transportation limit your teen's choice of summer program. Find the program and then find a solution.

ACADEMIC EXPECTATIONS

Although school may be closed, that doesn't mean that your child shouldn't crack a book over the next 10 weeks. Many schools send home a summer reading list for students. Still others require students to keep journals on their reading. *Whether your teen will be away for the summer or at home, whether she is pursuing an academic program or not, whether the school requires summer reading or not: you must.*

TIME TO SWITCH? MAYBE NOT

Many traditional summer camps offer programs for children between the ages of 8 and 15. So for the early adolescent, continuing to return to familiar stomping grounds as a camper may be not only right, but reassuring. (More about counselor-in-training programs follows.)

If your teen wants to return to camp, don't be too quick to insist on something new. Adolescence is difficult enough; the comfort of being with old camp friends may be just what your youngster needs.

Especially if he is not ready for a complicated social life—or is finding the social scene at home too stressful—camp may be a safe refuge for a few more years.

For the younger adolescent, the camp program should involve greater challenges and new activities that are age restricted to older campers. But you want your child to challenge himself. You want him to use the familiar setting, the old friends, to bolster his resolve to take new chances, assume more responsibility.

Talk to your camper before the summer begins about what he will do at camp this summer that will "stretch" him? Will he get his certification in life saving or CPR? Will he assume responsibility for the camp show? Lead the color war team? Swim across the lake? Learn to maintain the camp sailboats? Hike farther, longer? Develop wilderness skills? Whatever the camp offers, you are looking for your camper to set his own goals for the summer.

Counselor-in-Training/Waiter

Many summer camps offer 15- and 16-year-olds the opportunity to serve as junior counselors, sometimes called counselors-in-training (CIT). Some allow mid-teens to work as waiters or kitchen help. Generally, parents continue to pay tuition (sometimes at a reduced rate). The campers often receive a small stipend, gifts, or tips (if the camp permits) at the end of the summer. One parent was delighted that her son was eager to return to camp as a CIT. "It solved the whole question about the summer. I didn't have to worry about where he would be. I knew the camp was very strict about no smoking, drinking, or drugs, and I thought he would learn about working with kids. It was worth every penny, although several of his friends' parents wouldn't pay it."

If your teen has had a great time at camp, this is one way to continue the adventure. But you and your teen need to discuss with the camp director the duties and schedule of CITs or waiters. On the one hand you don't want to provide the camp with cheap labor who are saddled with too much responsibility. Nor do you want to overburden your child with duties inappropriate for his age. At the same time, if your teen chooses to spend his summer in this way, then you have to make clear that he is expected to act responsibly and to take his job seriously. The other side of the coin is that some CIT/waiter programs give the kids too much time off and too little supervision. When not on duty, there is no requirement to participate in the camp activities. Before enrolling your child in the program, check:

☼ What will be the teen's responsibilities?
☼ Who will supervise him when he is working and when he is off?
☼ Who will be his coworkers?
☼ What happens if he doesn't like his assignment?
☼ Do the teens participate in the regular camp activities?

There are advantages and disadvantages to participating in the program.

THE ADVANTAGES

☼ Camper returns to a familiar environment with friends.
☼ Camper has opportunity to learn responsibility and gain work experience.
☼ Work experience bolsters teen's résumé if he seeks counselor position in the future.
☼ Some camps increase salary of first-year counselors if they have participated in the CIT program.
☼ Assuming that camp has a good pre-camp training session, teen learns about working with children, techniques for handling problems, sensitivity training.
☼ Teen enrolled in safe, secure environment for summer.
☼ Most camps require teens to sign a pledge that forbids the use of alcohol, drugs, and tobacco and enforce these rules strictly.

THE DISADVANTAGES

☼ Parents must still pay camp fees (although maybe a reduced rate) even though teen is working.
☼ CITs/waiters may be underutilized or undersupervised.
☼ Teen may not take job seriously since his parents are paying for the experience.
☼ Teen returning to safe, familiar environment as opposed to trying something new.

SOMETHING DIFFERENT

But if your youngster is chafing at the bit to try something new; if you feel that the supervision or offerings at the camp are inadequate; if your youngster has "aged out" of his summer camp; if you believe that it's time that your teen earned some money—then the possibilities are endless. There are lots of choices: And over the teen years, your family may try several experiences. Your teen may decide to switch not because any one experience is bad, but because this is the age when the adventure of trying something new is half the fun.

The range of possibilities is limited only by imagination—and pocketbook. Among the alternatives are a wide variety of teen tours here and abroad; volunteer opportunities locally, nationally, abroad; academic programs; and jobs.

Focusing on *what* you want your teen to get from the summer experience is critical before you open the first glossy brochure. Even if cost is not a consideration, the most expensive program will not necessarily provide your child with the growth opportunities you are seeking for her. Furthermore, you've got to be realistic about teens in general—and your teen in particular. One mother who sent her slightly overweight daughter on an arduous bike tour, in hopes that it would improve her fitness, was shocked to discover that her daughter returned 20 pounds heavier! Snacks were readily available and a teen could opt out of the daily biking if she pleaded illness or fatigue—which her own daughter did frequently. The lessons learned from this experience are clear:

- ☼ Have realistic parental expectations of what a summer teen program can accomplish.
- ☼ Similarly, make sure that your teen doesn't expect the summer to transform her—it may, but you can't enter the program with those thoughts.
- ☼ Make sure that both parents and teen want to participate in the program. Enrolling a reluctant or unwilling adolescent is asking for problems. It's normal for adolescents to worry about new situations, but if they are doing the program just to please you, the possibility for disaster rises exponentially.

We'll discuss how to evaluate the programs/opportunities, and the pros and cons of each type of experience.

With or without Friends?

Whatever summer choice your teen makes, one of the questions that pops up again is: Should she go it alone or with a friend? Peer relationships are even more critical during adolescence and your child may be more willing to venture forth if accompanied by a friend. On the other hand, some teens welcome the opportunity to escape the "typecasting" that teens assign each other. The chance to reinvent yourself may be appealing.

The issues discussed in chapter 2 of whether or not to go to camp with a friend are still relevant. However, maturity and self-confidence that come with age may now permit your teen to reach out to new people even if accompanied to the program by a friend. Again, you and your teen must talk frankly and honestly about this issue.

Some programs are very strict about insisting that teens reach beyond the safety of the familiar. One hiking/camping program would not permit friends who had signed up together to bunk in the same tent. It forced both girls to reach out and make new friends—although they still enjoyed the security of beginning the program with a friend.

Check with the program director about how she encourages new friendships and minimizes the effect of cliques.

More School? Summer Academic Programs

Many public school systems, private schools, and colleges offer summer programs for enrichment or acceleration. Some programs are opportunities to explore a topic in more detail. For example, writing seminars give students a chance to focus in depth on style and creativity. Some programs are a combination of classroom work and field studies, for example, archaeological digs. Some programs offer tutoring for SATs. Some school systems will offer credit for academic classes taken during the summer. There are programs for every subject, in a wide range of academic disciplines and the arts.

To Find a Summer Academic Program

You need to decide if you want a local or residential program. Here are some ways to research good programs:

☀ Check local colleges, high schools, and private schools. These institutions often offer programs for enrichment, as well as remedial courses.

☀ Have your youngster register with the local youth employment program. In addition to jobs, many maintain a file on interesting summer programs, academics, and volunteer opportunities.

☼ Talk to favorite teachers or the guidance counselors for recommendations.

☼ Surf the Net, visiting the web sites of major colleges, universities, and prep schools for their summer offerings.

☼ Watch for the education supplements in major newspapers, such as the *New York Times*. They often carry articles and ads for summer academic programs for teens.

☼ Read guides such as *Peterson's Summer Opportunities for Kids and Teenagers* or *The College Board Summer on Campus* for academic programs. *Peterson's* also lists teen tours and nonacademic programs. (Check Appendix 5 for a list of other annual resource guides for summer jobs, volunteer opportunities, internships, and programs for teenagers.)

☼ *Remember:* Some programs rent classroom and dormitory space from universities and private schools without any relationship with the school other than tenant/landlord. Just because a program is offered on the campus of a university or private school does not mean that the courses are endorsed by the school or staffed by the institution's faculty.

Is an Academic Program Right for Your Student?

There are advantages and disadvantages to enrolling your teen in an academic program for the summer.

THE ADVANTAGES

☼ These classes are an opportunity to stretch intellectually or explore an area of study *without* the pressure of grades. If he does well, terrific. If he merely enjoys the experience, that's fine too.

☼ A student can earn a college degree in three years (reducing the cost of higher education) by taking Advanced Placement classes during the school year, and summer courses for credit.

☼ If it's a residential program, the student gets a preview of campus life.

☼ The more prestigious programs attract students from across the nation so the teen has the opportunity to meet a diverse group of adolescents.

☼ It may be an opportunity to accelerate in a specific subject. One student enrolled in an advanced math class over the summer in order to be able to enter the honors math program in the fall.

☼ It is a chance to take classes that are unavailable during the school year or that your student can't fit into her schedule.

☼ If desired, a student can take summer classes and accumulate enough credits to graduate early, up to a year, from high school. There are pluses and minuses to accelerating in high school, but if parents and student think it wise, this is one way to do it.

☼ If your child does well at a college-level program, he may ask the professor for a recommendation for college. It reflects well on his academic abilities that he has taken a challenging course and succeeded.

THE DISADVANTAGES

☼ It can build up unrealistic expectations about college in general and a specific school in particular. It's not unusual for a teen to believe that the summer program is representative of the college during the school year. But the summer student body and courses may have no connection to the type of students and courses offered on campus during the academic year. One high schooler spent the summer between her junior and senior year at an exciting summer program at a prestigious southern university. She insisted on applying early decision to the school, but was basing her choice on her summer experience.

Furthermore, summer on most college campuses is a gorgeous time, but again may not be representative of the academic year weather. As one admissions director ruefully pointed out, there's a reason why admissions offices only take pictures of college campuses in Maine during the spring and early fall!

Remember: these programs often just rent space from the schools where they are located.

☼ College admissions officers caution that taking a summer program at a university does not ensure, or even necessarily help, secure entrance to that school.

☼ If your student accelerates his studies during the summer, there may not be appropriate classes for him to take in the school year. For example, if he takes an advanced placement science class in the summer, will there be interesting science courses for him to take during the school year?

☼ Taking a summer academic program may be less of a challenge in some ways than trying a physically demanding trip or volunteering for a meaningful cause. For the good student, it's continuing what he already knows how to do—be a good student. For some academically strong students, school is probably the easiest choice, but choosing the easy way is not necessarily the smartest decision in this case.

☼ The summer program may offer little, if any, supervision of the students. Once the classes for the day are over, the student may be free to wander around until curfew—if there is a curfew. The maturity of your teen should determine his participation in this type of program.

HANDS UP: VOLUNTEER WORK

Your teen may not be interested in a teen tour, camp experience, or academic program. But he may gain a lot from volunteering his services. Some youngsters join an established program that provides interesting volunteer opportunities, both in the United States and abroad. Others create their own volunteer experience, finding a need within their own community and seeking to fill it. Although there is probably no pay for volunteer work, the rewards to your youngster (and the community) can be substantial.

Why volunteer? Kids learn a lot from donating their services. Your child will learn lessons he won't find in the classroom, but will have a direct impact on his educational experience—and his life. Again, think about the academic subjects your student must use in order to do his volunteer work effectively. Even the physical labor of mowing a shut-in's lawn requires fitness, time management, and judgment—all necessary skills for being a good student. But it also stretches his moral and ethical fiber to give to others. On a practical level, increasingly, schools are demanding some form of community service of students as a prerequisite for graduation.

Volunteer Opportunities for the Younger Teen

Younger teens can also provide service to their community. One way to fill an adolescent's summer is to establish a schedule for his volunteer jobs so he is busy at least part of every day. Most don't require leaving the community so the teen can become more independent and not have to rely on a parent for transportation. Here are some ways that even a 13-year-old can provide service:

☼ read to younger students
☼ clear sidewalks/rake leaves/mow lawns of neighborhood senior citizens
☼ beautification/environmental cleanup project
☼ run errands for the housebound
☼ bake or prepare treats or simple meals (with adult supervision) for those in need
☼ help (with adult supervision) at a soup kitchen or food pantry
☼ baby-sit or entertain the children of those attending meals at a soup kitchen or watch the children of the adult volunteers
☼ tutor

For the Older Teen

The more mature teen can go farther afield in search of a volunteer experience. In addition to the jobs above, there are several organizations that seek teens for volunteer opportunities. Some charge a fee for participation. (See Appendix 5 for addresses and web site information.)

☼ *Habitat for Humanity* has national and international placements in building homes for the needy.
☼ The *Student Conservation Association* has national placements for teens interested in the environment.
☼ The *Wesleyan Challenge* will fund selected community service projects designed by high school sophomores and juniors.
☼ *Volunteers for Peace* has international placements for teens interested in promoting world peace efforts.
☼ *Landmark Volunteers* places students in programs at historic trust sites in the United States.

Every community has needs that cry out for volunteers. Even if there isn't an established volunteer program, your teen can develop his own and offer his services to:

☼ local hospitals
☼ ambulance corps
☼ firehouse
☼ homeless shelters and soup kitchens
☼ literacy programs at the library

VOLUNTEER SERVICE AT HOME

One of the least explored opportunities for service is *service to the family*. It's so easy to search for ways to help the wider community and ignore the needs close at hand. For example, full-time care of an elderly grandparent is too much responsibility for a teen, but helping out on a part-time basis can be an enriching experience for both generations.

One high school junior volunteered one day a week to care for his elderly grandfather. The shopping, household chores, and gardening that were more than the senior citizen could handle on his own, were doable with the help of his grandson. The practical lessons that the teen learned from the older generation, like how to paint, grow vegetables, cook old family recipes, were irreplaceable. The emotional benefits for both grandfather and grandson were extraordinary.

WORKING FOR PAY

Paying jobs can be a great learning experience, give your student a little financial independence, and teach the old-fashioned standards about dependability and reliability. While teens are often ready and eager for work experience, jobs may be hard to find. Most states require younger teens (under 16) to get working papers in order to hold a job.

How old should your student be before she gets a job? By the time your student is in seventh grade, she can begin looking for one of the traditional first jobs that most parents remember from their own early adolescence: baby-sitter/mother's helper, snow shoveler, lawn care, pet sitter, golf caddy.

Encourage your child to be a little creative in landing jobs. One seventh grader used the graphics program on his home computer to develop a flyer advertising his lawn care service. He distributed the flyer throughout the neighborhood and lined up enough jobs to fill five summer mornings. That still left the afternoons free to "hang out" with his buddies.

One enterprising high schooler took the desktop publishing skills he learned from working on his school newspaper, and parlayed them into a freelance job creating newsletters for local businesses. His pay? Twenty dollars per hour!

Work Rules for Kids

If your student is 14 or over and wants to get a job, he may need to get a work permit (required in most states). Generally you can get working papers from the school guidance office. To apply, he will need to get your permission (usually on a standard form), as well as proof of age.

Federal child labor laws limit the number of hours a 14- or 15-year-old can work.

☆ no more than three hours on a school day or 18 hours in a school week

☆ no more than eight hours on a nonschool day or 40 hours in a nonschool week

☆ not before 7 A.M. or after 7 P.M., except during the summer when they can work until 9 P.M.

There may be other state laws that apply.

Develop *Marketable* Skills

Teens who want to get paying jobs in the summer need to plan ahead. Encourage your adolescent to think about summer jobs *before* school

RÉSUMÉ-BUILDING FOR COLLEGE

Most colleges ask applicants about their summer activities. When choosing a program for your high school student, consider how it will reflect and develop his interests and abilities. This doesn't mean that he can't hold a paying job (that develops his independence and teaches important skills as well). But a strong summer program may be a way to clearly demonstrate to a college an applicant's interest in a specific field. For example, one high school junior, who thought he wanted to be a doctor, took a summer job at a local restaurant (for pay), but also volunteered at the local hospital, as well as joining his town's volunteer ambulance corps. It made for a busy summer, but the student got valuable exposure in the medical field, as well as earning spending money.

In another twist, one student who worked in a dry cleaning business wrote his college essay about the customers he met, the lives they led, the lessons he learned. A quiet summer can have an enormous impact.

ends, so he has the time to take any necessary courses or certification he will need in order to be hired. For example, one teen job that pays well is working as a lifeguard. There is always an enormous demand for qualified life guards: the town pool/beach, apartment complexes, private clubs, and day camps are all looking for this seasonal help. *But* your teen will need her lifeguard certification in order to apply. Check with your local Red Cross, recreation department, or Y, to see when they are offering lifesaving certification courses. Teens often use their spring vacation to take an intensive course to get certification.

Similarly, have your teen brush up on his word processing skills or learn a new computer program (such as for spreadsheets or desktop publishing), so that his résumé includes attractive office skills.

Where to Find a Job

Finding a job for a teenager is tough. There are the traditional ones such as camp counselor, mother's helper, office temps, lawn work. But for the under-18 adolescent, finding meaningful or interesting summer employment is difficult. But that's not to say it's not worth the effort. Here are some good leads.

※ newspaper ads
※ the youth employment office or high school guidance department
※ office temp businesses
※ college and community bulletin boards
※ old-fashioned footwork: visit local businesses, offices, private clubs and *ask*
※ family friends/parents of friends

Encourage your teen to begin looking for a summer job at least by May, if not before. In fact, if he can work part-time before the summer begins, he may get a leg up on the competition. And if a student is willing to continue on a part-time basis during the school year, he may be a more attractive job applicant.

How Much Work Is Too Much?

Keep a careful eye on how much your teen works. Researchers at Stanford and Temple Universities found that students who worked more than 20 hours a week during the school year were more likely:

BORING MAY BE BETTER

And here's an interesting concept. A boring summer job may be just what the doctor ordered to help a teen get focused on the value of education. One mother tells an apocryphal summer job story. Her son, a mediocre student, though bright, had always wanted to work at the local gas station. Finally, he got a summer job and the first day, the owner gave him a putty knife and had him scrape the floor. The summer was hard, boring, and frustrating, but that fall, the student's grades had never been better! He actually confessed to his mother that he had learned that he "never wanted to do that kind of work again."

☼ to have lower grades because they have less time to devote to their studies

☼ to be more detached from their parents because they have less time to devote to family activities

☼ to have a higher rate of alcohol and drug use because they have more discretionary income

Remind your student that his full-time job is school. Make sure that your student:

☼ does not cut corners academically in order to work

☼ does not take fewer challenging courses in order to relieve academic pressures

☼ does not sacrifice other extracurricular activities. While the job is terrific, it should not be her sole outside activity.

Too Young for Networking?

Should you help your teen get a job? Why not? But there are limits to what a parent should do to secure their teen summer employment.

Remember: *The process of getting a job is as important a learning experience as the job itself.*

There is nothing wrong with helping your teen develop a résumé or introducing your teen to a family friend or business acquaintance who may need summer help. *But let the teen take it from there.* He should fill out the application, make the appointment for a job interview, figure out logistics for how to get to the job (even if that means asking for transportation help), and, of course, work responsibly while employed.

TEEN TOURS AND ADVENTURES

Biking, hiking, sailing, rafting, spelunking, wind surfing, rock climbing, diving, trail blazing, sight-seeing—the summer opportunities for teen trips and adventures are virtually endless. Should you sign up your adolescent for this type of adventure? Maybe. There are, as with any summer opportunity, advantages and disadvantages.

ADVANTAGES

☀ An opportunity to visit and explore new places and meet new people.

☀ Tours may offer teens unique physical and intellectual challenges, or even just try new tasks.

☀ Teens learn responsibility for self and belongings. Some trips require greater obligations, for example, the participants are responsible for cooking meals.

☀ Trips may expose teens to places and experiences they otherwise wouldn't have. For example, one mother was delighted that her son went on a six-week biking/camping trip because she said she knew that they would never as a family go on that kind of adventure. "I've no interest in biking 40 miles a day, but my son does."

☀ Finishing programs, especially demanding physical ones, builds self-esteem and self-confidence that carry over to other parts of teen's life.

☀ Learn group dynamics and cooperation as adolescents are thrown together and must learn to cope with each other over the course of the trip. That is true even if some of the teens are more difficult. One father pointed out that "my son learned on a biking trip that he didn't have to necessarily like someone in order to have to learn how to work cooperatively."

☀ Teens may enjoy greater freedom and independence within the context of a supervised program.

☀ Teens may develop lifelong friendships on these kinds of programs. The close quarters and shared experiences encourage intense friendships.

DISADVANTAGES

☼ Tours are expensive. Economics may limit the diversity of the participants.

☼ There may be too little supervision.

☼ Some tours are more a social exercise than a challenge intellectually or physically.

Is Your Teen Ready for a Tour?

But even before you get down to the nitty-gritty of choosing among the thousands of programs, before you figure out how much you are willing to spend for this adventure, you need to be realistic about your teen's personality and readiness. It can make the difference between a summer of enormous growth or a potential disaster.

1. **First big question: Does your teen want to go on this type of trip?** If your teen is only a lukewarm participant in this experience, perhaps you need to look for some other summer activity. These trips are too expensive and too demanding for someone who is doing it only to please her family. That is not to say that your teen may not be apprehensive about the program—that's not unusual. But you want to hear that your child is looking forward to the challenge and interested in the planned program.

   But this requires you to match the trip to your child's personality and interests. It's silly to spend the time and money on a program that your child will find a complete bore. One teen was unhappy with her cross-country trip because the tour spent too much time in amusement parks! Other kids loved it, but you have to know your child.

2. **Is your teen flexible?** This is probably the most important characteristic in determining your child's adjustment and enjoyment of a teen tour. These programs are fairly demanding physically—even if the teen isn't backpacking through the Rockies, but instead is on a charter bus tour of the Northwest. The program's schedule changes every day. If it's Tuesday it must be Belgium. . . . If your teen tends to be a homebody, if she finds travel and change difficult, if it takes her a long time to adjust to new situations and new people, then these kinds of tours may be more difficult and less enjoyable. It's not to say that a shy, tentative type can't enjoy a teen tour, but you certainly

want to discuss your child's personality with the tour directors. It may be that a smaller group tour or one of shorter duration would be a better choice.

3. **Can your child meet the physical demands of the trip?** This is just being realistic. Don't expect a physically demanding tour to be the answer for curing the couch potato. Kids on these types of tours have little patience for those who can't keep up. If it's going to be a lot of hiking, biking, or camping, make sure your teen is willing, eager to participate, and in good enough shape.

On a more practical level, if your teen tends to suffer from motion sickness, consider carefully the type of program you choose. Long bus tours, even in luxurious coaches, can still be trying for the individual who is prone to motion sickness.

4. **Is your teen mature and responsible enough to handle the independence of a teen tour?** The most extensive teen tours are really slated for the 15- and 16-year-olds, but chronological age is not the most important gauge. How mature is your teen's decision making? Can she withstand peer pressure? One mother opted not to send her daughter on a well-known European teen tour because trip participants were free to tour Paris and Amsterdam in small groups without any adult supervision. Many parents complain that some programs offer teens greater freedom than they have at home. You need to know your child and how she will react to this kind of freedom—and what her response will be if she sees other tour participants act irresponsibly.

5. **Is she organized?** Your teen will be responsible for packing and unpacking. Will most, if not all, of her clothing and belongings make it home after weeks of moving from one place to another?

HOW TO CHOOSE

It can be daunting to try and choose among the myriad of teen tours and programs. You can begin to narrow the search by deciding first:

1. How much can you spend.

2. How long can your teen be away.

3. How far do you want your teen to travel from home.

THE TRUTH ABOUT DRUGS AND ALCOHOL

Teen tours, as a rule, enforce a strict code prohibiting the use of drugs and alcohol by teen participants. Most require teens and parents to sign a contract that spells out the penalty for drug or alcohol use—immediate expulsion and forfeiture of all fees.

That said, the truth is that sometimes kids break the rules. A survey of parents whose children have participated in these programs reveals that these types of incidents do occur. In most cases, the tour leaders followed up swiftly and enforced the contract immediately. Offenders were not given second chances. But there are also stories of teens who weren't caught or were let off the hook by more lenient counselors.

Parents need to talk to their child about drugs and alcohol before they leave on a teen tour. Even if your adolescent rolls his eyes and indicates he's heard this lecture a thousand times before—spell it out again.

1. Talk about peer pressure and the increased freedom he will have on this tour.

2. Let him know that you believe in him and trust he will use good judgment.

3. Make it clear that *you* will not tolerate any drug or alcohol use and that there will be serious consequences, above and beyond whatever the tour group does, if there is a problem.

Budget

Teen tours can run between $2,000 and $10,000, when all is said and done. For example, a 28-day, four-country European trip (including the French Riviera!) costs $5,695, plus airfare, and that doesn't even cover spending money and souvenirs.

Other programs are shorter and less expensive, but there is little financial aid available for these trips, so budget has to be the first question you answer.

Time Available

You may want or need a trip of a certain length. Look at the entire summer and budget your teen's time—and the family's time as well since you may want to plan a family vacation. For example, one 15-year-old went on a teen tour that was built around hiking and camping in the Pacific Northwest. When she returned home, she attended week-long local sports clinics in lacrosse and tennis. The following year, her family took a week vacation, next she spent a month at Amherst College in an academic program, then she returned home and fulfilled her community service obligation at a local environmental program, and again attended the sports clinics—a full summer indeed.

How Far?

Time and money may limit how far your teen can travel. But even if not, it's important to understand your teen's personal preferences—as well as your own. If your child is hesitant to go out of the country or even across the country on a teen trip, look for another program. With the wide range of trips from which to choose, there is probably one that travels the right distance, fills the right amount of time (although not necessarily at the right price).

What Else Do You Want?

Having made the decision that a teen tour is right, begin your search using the same methods as you did to find a summer camp: word of mouth, web searches, guidance counselors, camp adviser, ads, camp fairs, resource books (see Appendix 5).

Narrow your search by the type of tour you want: city or country; indoors or out? If your teen is interested and up to the challenge of camping out—then you can focus on the more outdoor adventures. If camping means the local motel rather than a four-star resort—then you have to know that too. If your teen never met a rock he didn't like, that steers you in one direction. If your child is more interested in malls than mountains, museums than streams, then you know that you are searching for something else.

Don't try to turn your teen into something she's not. That doesn't mean you can't expose her to new opportunities and adventures, but it's unrealistic to think that she will enjoy a 28-day camping trip if she has never shown any interest in the outdoors. That's not to say she won't survive—but that is probably not the purpose of the program.

The Nitty-Gritty

For each program you research, you need to know:

GROUP SIZE AND ORGANIZATION

How many teens are on the tour?

How many adults?

If the tour is broken into smaller groups, how many teens are in each group, with what kind of supervision?

Do the groups stay together the whole trip or does the director reorganize the groups during the tour to encourage friendships and avoid cliques?

What is the age range of the participants? It should be only a year or two because the maturity and interests of a younger teen are not the same as an older high schooler.

If coed, do girls get the same opportunities as boys? Are responsibilities on camping trips assigned without gender bias? How do the leaders handle trip romances?

METHOD OF TRANSPORTATION

How does the trip travel from one site to another: bus, train, car, plane, hiking, biking, rafting?

How far does the trip travel in any one day?

If by bus, what kind of coach? Are there bathrooms on board?

If by bike, raft, or on foot, what happens if there is bad weather? If a teen doesn't feel well?

If by train or plane, does the group sit together? What kind of planes do they use (commercial or charter? jet or propeller?)

LIVING ACCOMMODATIONS

What kind of accommodations: hotels, tents, dorms, youth hostels? (Ask for specifics so you can check out the accommodations yourself in your own guide books.)

What kind of supervision is there once the group is in the housing? Are there leaders on every floor?

If a coed tour, are girls and boys assigned to separate floors? What kind of supervision is there?

CURFEWS

How are the rules enforced?

Are there room checks? When? By whom?

SPENDING MONEY

How much?

Is the teen responsible for carrying the money?

What is best: cash, traveler's checks, or credit cards?

What if the teen runs out? Are there emergency loans or advances from the tour?

Do any kind of controls exist on how the money is spent?

What do most participants buy during the trip?

TOUR LEADERS

How long has the company been in business?

What are the credentials of the chaperons of each trip? How old are the chaperons? (They should be at least college graduates in order to have the experience and maturity needed to supervise adolescents.)

How often has the company been running the specific tour that interests your teen?

SUPERVISION

This is a critical issue. It's not just a question of how many chaperons are on the trip, but how closely they supervise the youngsters. Some programs permit the teens to tour the city, mall, amusement park unaccompanied, meeting at an agreed upon place at the end of the day. Others accompany each group from site to site. You want to know *before* you enroll your child the trip policy on supervision.

MEDICAL EMERGENCIES

Inevitably, someone gets sick on every tour—usually minor illnesses that are easily treated. Sometimes it's just the exhaustion of the tour, and the teen sleeps in or takes the bus instead of biking or hiking.

Ask for specifics about how the tour handles an emergency if not in a metropolitan area (on a camping trip, for example).

How will the parents be notified if an emergency arises?

Will the leaders insist on a plastic surgeon if stitches are required?

Can a teen rejoin the tour if hurt? For example, one teen broke her arm while on a hiking trip. After a few days away from the trip for treatment, she rejoined (and enjoyed) the rest of the tour.

MAIL/COMMUNICATION HOME

How and when can you communicate with your child?

Are there any restrictions on calls or mail? Some tours don't permit parents to write, although the teen can call or write anytime. This is because on an outdoor adventure program, coordinating mail drops can be cumbersome.

If there are mail restrictions, how does the trip handle birthdays? One mother accepted the "no mail" rule, but asked if she could send a package to her daughter on her birthday. No problem, replied the tour leaders who worked out the logistics with the family.

How will your child call home: calling card, prepaid phone card, collect?

If you plan to give your teen a phone card to use to call home, shop around for the best rates—they vary tremendously, even within the same company. One family discovered that calling their son, who was in an academic program in Scotland, cost 12 cents a minute, but when he called them using the phone card they gave him, the rate was $1.14 a minute. By comparing rates among various long-distance companies, the family was able to find a deal that charged 12 cents a minute whether the parents dialed direct or the son called using the phone card. *However*, the rate was effective only for dialing one single designated number (in this case, home). When the son used the calling card to phone any other number in the United States (friends, his grandmother), the rate was again $1.14 a minute. Make clear to your teen when and with whom he can use the phone card.

For wilderness/outdoor trips, what kind of communication setup do leaders have for emergencies?

MEALS

How many meals are part of the plan? One European teen tour provided breakfast and dinner, but the teens were responsible for getting their own lunches. Imagine the sticker shock one parent felt when she got a credit card bill for a $300 lunch her teen enjoyed at a four-star restaurant in Paris! Assuming your child won't be eating quite so well, ask for details about the meals. How often does the tour hit fast-food restaurants? It's the easy way out for feeding teens, but not the healthiest. Whatever restaurants the tour frequents, can teens choose off the menu or is the meal planned? How much choice in meals do the participants have? What about teens with special diets or preferences (vegetarians)?

For those programs where the teens cook the meals, how elaborate is the menu? How much help do they get? In one case, a teenage boy who enjoyed cooking was frankly incensed at the pedestrian nature of the meals he was expected to cook.

EQUIPMENT

For bike, spelunking, rafting, snorkeling, and hiking trips, ask who provides the equipment. Do they use/recommend a specific brand of equipment? If you are expected to provide the bike, in what form? Who puts the bike together? Some trips require a certain model that can withstand the rigors of the junket. How are repairs handled once the trip has begun?

LAUNDRY

Who is responsible? How often is it done? As one father pointed out: "It was painfully clear when he came home that his laundry had never been done during the two-week bike trip from Seattle to San Francisco."

CHECK IT OUT

It's critically important to invest the time in a thorough evaluation of each of these programs. You can't rely on the brochures, videos, or even the rec-

---

TIP:

Ask the parent if she knows anyone who was not satisfied with the program. When one mother asked that question, the other family volunteered the name and phone number of another trip participant who had not enjoyed the program. Needless to say, the tour operators had not provided this family as a reference. It turned out that it was a matter of parenting style—one family felt the supervision had been too lax, the other felt it had been appropriate.

---

ommendations of a camp/trip adviser. You have to call the parents of previous participants and ask tough questions before you enroll your child.

Good trips will provide you with references of participants from the previous year. You want recent participants because the trip and leadership may have changed over the years. One mother advised calling several, up to 10 families, in order to be sure that you have gotten a broad range of opinions. Calling just one or two families may mean that complaints may be specific to those individuals. But if you hear an issue raised enough times, it's a clear sign that you should raise the point with the tour leaders.

For example, one mother was concerned with the description, offered by several references, of the supervision on a tour she was considering for her child. She thought it sounded too lax. When she asked the tour leaders, they agreed that the description of their policies was accurate, but they believed their approach was appropriate for that age group.

> **Remember**: It's not necessarily a question of right or wrong, but a decision about what you are comfortable with for your child.

Ask to speak to the parent when calling for a reference. Speaking with the teen who participated in a recent trip may be helpful, especially for your own child, but you want an adult's perspective on the supervision and overall value of the trip. Ask about supervision, money matters, meals, cliques, etc., and then probe a little deeper. As any good interviewer knows, don't be afraid of a little silence. Often if you don't respond immediately, the other person will expand on their original answer and give more details.

What Your Teen Needs to Know

Before your teenager leaves for her first trip/tour, you need to review several issues. Some are topics that you've talked about before (peer pressure, sex), but it's still important to review them again. Consider that she is away from home, in a new situation, with a new group, with perhaps more freedom than she has ever enjoyed before: In that context it's time for a talk!

PEER PRESSURE

Okay, you've reviewed the perennial: "If everyone jumped off the Empire State Building, would you?" but you need to put it in perspective for your teen. Adolescent peer pressure can be intense, especially when the teenager is with a new group of peers and doesn't want to appear like a wimp or nerd.

Talk about the issues of drugs, alcohol, sex, breaking curfew. Point out that pranks that seem innocent can be potentially dangerous or illegal; for example, sneaking out to swim in the motel pool at midnight; stealing towels; using a forbidden hot plate. You are asking your child to use her best judgment—and to step back when the excitement of the moment with friends tempts her to do something she knows is wrong, dangerous, illegal—or all three.

These kinds of trips are also the moment when some adolescents decide to pierce ears (or other body parts), bleach hair, get tattoos, etc. Talk about the need to think through decisions before rushing into them in the heat of the moment or on a dare. "Will I still like this choice six months from now," is not a bad way to put any decision into perspective.

SEX

By the time your child is an adolescent, you've probably had several conversations about sex. But before she goes away, it's smart to talk about it again. Don't be worried that it will seem like you are suggesting that sex is part of teen tours. Generally, like coed dorms at college, the teen tour groups tend to develop close friendships rather than romances. There is a brother/sister quality to these relationships. But, of course, there are still some teens who develop a romance while traveling. Talk about personal values, responsibility, and caution.

MONEY

Learning to budget money is a valuable lesson that can be learned on a teen trip. The spending money you give before your child leaves needs to last the length of the program. Help your child learn some financial planning and budget skills before the trip.

1. Have your teen develop a list of her anticipated expenses and how she plans to allocate her money. Build in a reserve fund for unexpected expenses.

2. Discuss how your teen will carry the money. A fanny pack is preferable to handbags or just a back pocket, both of which are more susceptible to pickpockets.

3. Review tipping customs (practice on restaurant bills before your teen leaves). You want him to understand that youth does not excuse cheapness—waiters, bellhops, taxi drivers, all depend on tips.

4. Remind your teen to double-check the addition of bills in stores and restaurants, and not be embarrassed about pointing out errors.

5. Tell your teenager not to "flash his cash." Keep money discreet.

6. Review what are appropriate uses of a credit card, if you plan to give one to your child. Remember, away from the community, using a credit card to get cash from an ATM may trigger service charges. A teen may get $20 and not realize that fees tack on an extra $4.

COMMUNICATION

Agree with your teen how often he will call or write home. The problem with setting a specific time to call is that your teenager may not necessarily be near a phone at that time; on the other hand, without a general idea of when he will call, you could end up with two weeks of messages on the answering machine. Check with the tour leaders for advice on specific days and times.

Even if your teenager is not much of a correspondent, if the trip permits mail, continue to write. Kids need that link to home. The trip leaders will provide an itinerary and the correct mailing addresses. Mark letters and packages: Hold for (Name of Tour) Trip.

If you are giving your child a prepaid phone card or access to your telephone calling card, agree on how it can be used. Can she call friends as well as family? Remember, each prepaid phone card has a preset number of minutes. If she uses them up calling friends, she will have to spend money or call collect to speak to you.

PACKING

It's especially important to teach your teenager how to pack and unpack efficiently. He will be responsible for his own belongings on this trip. Strewing clothes on the hotel floor increases the likelihood of something getting left behind. Even the sloppiest or most disorganized teen needs to understand that Mom will not be there to be make sure that he hasn't left behind his hiking boots or favorite shirt.

Have him pack his own duffel/suitcase/backpack for the trip. Make a list of what he is taking. Keep one copy at home and let him take one on the trip. That way he can check off if he has all his belongings at each stop.

Follow the suggestions or recommendations of the trip leaders on the type and amount of clothing. Clothes that need ironing or special care should be left at home. And you may want to advise your teen on the special care and protection her belongings may require depending on the location of the trip. The camping trip in the Pacific Northwest was so incredibly damp that one mother couldn't fathom how her daughter ever had a dry piece of clothing to put on in the mornings. Her daughter discovered that lining her backpack with plastic garbage bags kept out the dampness.

LAUNDRY

Review laundry basics with your teen before he leaves. But as one mother pointed out: "It's not that I didn't explain how to do wash to my son. He just chose not to. I've never seen such black clothes—or feet for that matter—as I saw when he returned from his bike tour. I ended up literally throwing out all his clothes." Make your expectations and his responsibilities for basic hygiene as clear as possible.

COMING HOME

Teen reentry into the household can be a little tricky. Remember he's been living a much more independent life for the last few weeks and may chafe at the family rules. Without giving up your standards, try to use gentle, never sarcastic, humor rather than anger when confronting your seemingly belligerent teen.

Remember too that one of the reasons you sent your teen on a trip was to build his self-confidence and independence. Don't be surprised if the trip accomplished these goals and now your teenager wants to exercise some of that hard-won independence at home. If he has earned your trust and shows good judgment, it may be time to relax some of the rules. Part of parenting an adolescent is gradually letting go.

Often, you'll notice that your phone bills take a significant jump when your teen returns from his summer activity. The friends he met may live at a distance. But as one mother pointed out, the friend her 14-year-old met on a biking tour of New England remains one his closest friends 10 years later. The very diversity you thought was so attractive about the trip in the first place may be reflected in subsequent higher telephone bills.

Your teenager may also spend more hours on-line, communicating by e-mail with far-flung friends—and planning reunions and the next trip.

Your child's adolescence can be a trying—and rewarding—period for you both. Choosing the right summer program can be a help. If your child spends at least part of the summer away from home, it may give you both a necessary respite from the trials of his growing up. If spent at home, it may give you an opportunity to see another side of him as he assumes the responsibility of working, volunteerism, or serious study. Whatever the choice, remember that no matter what signals he sends, your teenager needs you now more than ever. Support and guide his summer choice so that it provides him with the opportunities for growth, emotionally, socially, physically, and intellectually, that he needs.

Appendix 1

Day Camp Evaluation Sheet

Name of Camp _____

Director _____

Address _____

Fax _____

E-mail _____

Accreditation? _____

Recommended by:_____

Length of Session

1 week _____ 2 weeks _____ 4 weeks _____ 7/8 weeks _____ Other _____

Camp Fee _____

Visit

On-site _____ Home Visit by Director/Representative _____ Video _____

Camp Organization

_____ Number of children in each age group

_____ Number of counselors for each age group

_____ Staff/Camper Ratio

Health and Safety Checklist

Nurse(s) on-site? _____

Closest hospital? _____

Does the camp maintain a strict immunization policy? _____

Who on the staff is trained in CPR? _____

Are emergency fire drills held? _____

Are there smoke detectors in all buildings? _____

Are all visitors screened before entering camp? _____

How is traffic around the camp organized? _____

Rainy Day Facilities?_____

Activities Available (also note if taught by specialist or by bunk counselor)

   Team Sports

   _____ Baseball

   _____ Basketball

   _____ Field Hockey

_____ Football
_____ Hockey
     _____ Ice
     _____ Rollerblades
_____ Lacrosse
_____ Soccer
_____ Softball
_____ Volleyball

Individual Sports

_____ Archery
_____ Biking
     _____ Minibikes
_____ Fencing
_____ Fishing
_____ Go-carts
_____ Golf
_____ Gymnastics
_____ Martial Arts
_____ Riding
_____ Squash
_____ Tennis
_____ Track/Field
_____ Wrestling

Waterfront

_____ Canoeing
_____ Diving
_____ Jetskiing
_____ Kayaking
_____ Motor Boat
_____ Sailing
_____ Scuba
_____ Swimming
_____ Waterskiing
_____ Windsurfing

Arts and Crafts

_____ Basketry
_____ Batik
_____ Candle-making
_____ Jewelry
_____ Leatherwork
_____ Metalwork

_____ Painting
_____ Pottery/Ceramics
_____ Stained Glass
_____ Tie-Dyeing
_____ Weaving
_____ Woodworking

Performing Arts

_____ Acting
_____ Costuming
_____ Dance
 _____ Ballet
 _____ Choreography
 _____ Creative Movement
 _____ Folk Dance
 _____ Jazz
 _____ Modern Dance
_____ Directing
_____ Lighting
_____ Magic
_____ Makeup
_____ Music
 _____ Instrumental
 _____ Orchestra/Band _____ Chorus
 _____ Practice Time Set
 _____ Private Lessons Available
 _____ Voice
_____ Photography
_____ Puppetry
_____ Set Construction
_____ Radio
_____ Video

Other

_____ Computers
_____ Ecology
_____ Farm Animals
_____ Gardening
_____ Marine Biology
_____ Nature Study
_____ Rocketry

General Comments and Observations _____

_____

Appendix 2

Overnight Camp Evaluation Sheet

Name of Camp _____

Director _____

Address _____

Telephone _____

Fax_____

E-mail _____

Accreditation? _____

Recommended by:_____

Type of Camp

Coed _____ All Boys _____ All Girls _____

Religious Affiliation _____

Uniform Required _____

Length of Session

1 week _____ 2 weeks _____ 4 weeks _____ 7/8 weeks _____ Other _____

Camp Fee _____

Visit

On-site _____ Home Visit by Director/Representative _____ Video _____

Parents' Visiting Day

Date _____

Children remain on-site? _____

Camp Organization

_____ Number of children in each age group

_____ Number of children in each bunk

_____ Number of counselors for each bunk

_____ Staff/Camper Ratio

Health and Safety Checklist

Infirmary

Doctor on-site? _____

Nurse(s) on-site? _____

Infirmary on-site? _____ # of beds _____

Closest hospital? _____

Does the camp maintain a strict immunization policy? _____

Who on staff is trained in CPR? _____

Are emergency fire drills held? _____

Are there smoke detectors in all buildings? _____

Are all visitors screened before entering camp? _____

How is traffic around the camp organized? _____

Bunks

Construction of bunks

             Wooden Building _____ Air-conditioned? _____

             Tents _____

Toilets in bunks? _____

Showers in bunks? _____

Rainy Day Facilities? _____

_____

Activities Available (also note if taught by specialist or by bunk counselor)

Team Sports

_____ Baseball

_____ Basketball

_____ Field Hockey

_____ Football

_____ Hockey

        _____ Ice

        _____ Rollerblades

_____ Lacrosse

_____ Soccer

_____ Softball

_____ Volleyball

Individual Sports

_____ Archery

_____ Biking

        _____ Minibikes

_____ Fencing

_____ Fishing

_____ Go-carts

_____ Golf

_____ Gymnastics

_____ Martial Arts

_____ Riding

_____ Squash
_____ Tennis
_____ Track/Field
_____ Wrestling

Waterfront
_____ Canoeing
_____ Diving
_____ Jetskiing
_____ Kayaking
_____ Motor Boat
_____ Sailing
_____ Scuba
_____ Swimming
_____ Waterskiing
_____ Windsurfing

Arts and Crafts
_____ Basketry
_____ Batik
_____ Candle-making
_____ Jewelry
_____ Leatherwork
_____ Metalwork
_____ Painting
_____ Pottery/Ceramics
_____ Stained Glass
_____ Tie-Dyeing
_____ Weaving
_____ Woodworking

Performing Arts
_____ Acting
_____ Costuming
_____ Dance
    _____ Ballet
    _____ Choreography
    _____ Creative Movement
    _____ Folk Dance
    _____ Jazz
    _____ Modern Dance
_____ Directing
_____ Lighting

_____ Magic
_____ Makeup
_____ Music
      _____ Instrumental
      _____ Orchestra/Band _____ Chorus
      _____ Practice Time Set
      _____ Private Lessons Available
      _____ Voice
_____ Photography
_____ Puppetry
_____ Radio
_____ Set Construction
_____ Video

Other
_____ Computers
_____ Ecology
_____ Farm Animals
_____ Gardening
_____ Marine Biology
_____ Nature Study
_____ Rocketry

General Comments and Observations _____

_____

Appendix 3

Special Interest/Special Needs Camp Evaluation Sheet

Name of Camp _____
Director _____
Address _____
Telephone _____
Fax_____
E-mail _____
Accreditation? _____
Recommended by:_____

Length of Session
1 week _____ 2 weeks _____ 4 weeks _____ 7/8 weeks _____ Other _____

Camp Fee _____

Visit
On-site _____ Home Visit by Director/Representative _____ Video _____

Camp Organization
_____ Number of children in each age group
_____ Number of counselors for each age group
_____ Staff/Camper Ratio

Health and Safety Checklist
Doctor on-site? _____
Nurse(s) on-site? _____
Closest hospital? _____
Other medical information: _____
_____
Specialists (medical, educational) on staff: _____
_____
Are emergency fires drills held?_____
Are there smoke detectors in all buildings? _____
Are all visitors screened before entering camp? _____
How is traffic around the camp organized? _____

Rainy Day Facilities? _____
_____

Activities Available (also note if taught by specialist or by bunk counselor)

Team Sports
_____ Baseball
_____ Basketball
_____ Field Hockey
_____ Football
_____ Hockey
     _____ Ice
     _____ Rollerblades
_____ Lacrosse
_____ Soccer
_____ Softball
_____ Volleyball

Individual Sports
_____ Archery
_____ Biking
     _____ Minibikes
_____ Fencing
_____ Fishing
_____ Go-carts
_____ Golf
_____ Gymnastics
_____ Martial Arts
_____ Riding
_____ Squash
_____ Tennis
_____ Track/Field
_____ Wrestling

Waterfront
_____ Canoeing
_____ Diving
_____ Jetskiing
_____ Kayaking
_____ Motor Boat
_____ Sailing
_____ Scuba
_____ Swimming
_____ Waterskiing
_____ Windsurfing

Arts and Crafts
_____ Basketry
_____ Batik
_____ Candle-making
_____ Jewelry

_____ Leatherwork
_____ Metalwork
_____ Painting
_____ Pottery/Ceramics
_____ Stained Glass
_____ Tie-Dyeing
_____ Weaving
_____ Woodworking

Performing Arts
_____ Acting
_____ Costuming
_____ Dance
        _____ Ballet
        _____ Choreography
        _____ Creative Movement
        _____ Folk Dance
        _____ Jazz
        _____ Modern Dance
_____ Directing
_____ Lighting
_____ Magic
_____ Makeup
_____ Music
        _____ Instrumental
        _____ Orchestra/Band _____ Chorus
        _____ Practice Time Set
        _____ Private Lessons Available
        _____ Voice
_____ Photography
_____ Puppetry
_____ Radio
_____ Set Construction
_____ Video

Other
_____ Computers
_____ Ecology
_____ Farm Animals
_____ Gardening
_____ Marine Biology
_____ Nature Study
_____ Rocketry

General Comments and Observations _____

_____

Appendix 4

Packing List for Four Weeks at Sleepaway Camp

Mark *every* item with name of camper

Recommended Quantity	Clothing	# Packed for Camp	# Returned Home
14	T-shirts		
1	Light sweater/sweatshirt		
10	Shorts		
2	Jeans		
4	Sweatpants		
4	Swimsuits		
1	Light pajamas		
1	Heavy pajamas		
1	Terry cloth bathrobe		
14	Pairs of underpants		
21	Pairs of socks		
1	Belt		
Footwear			
1	Sneakers (tennis)		
1	Basketball sneakers		
1	Sandals, rubber thongs		
1	Waterproof shoes		
1	Slippers		
1	Soccer cleats		
1	Hiking boots		
Optional:	Dance footwear, aerobic footwear, Rollerblades		
Linens			
2	Blankets		
2	Fitted sheets (cot size)		
2	Flat sheets (cot size)		
2	Pillow cases		
1	Pillow		
10	Towels		
2	Washcloths		
1	Shower caddy/Dobb kit (including soap dish, toothbrush holder, collapsible cup)		
1	Laundry bag		

Recommended Quantity	Clothing	# Packed for Camp	# Returned Home
Athletic Equipment			
1	Baseball glove	_____	_____
1	Tennis racquet	_____	_____
3	Cans of tennis balls	_____	_____
1	Shin guards	_____	_____
1	Mouth guard	_____	_____
1	Athletic supporter with cup (boys)	_____	_____
Optional:	Rollerblade safety equipment (knee, elbow, wrist guards, helmet); golf clubs; fishing gear	_____	_____
Outdoor Gear			
1	Hooded poncho	_____	_____
1	Heavy jacket	_____	_____
1	Lightweight jacket	_____	_____
1	Sleeping bag	_____	_____
1	Flashlight	_____	_____
1	Canteen	_____	_____
Packing			
1	Trunk with lock	_____	_____
1	Duffel with lock	_____	_____
Personal Items			
	Camera and film	_____	_____
	Stationery/stamps	_____	_____
	Pens and pencils	_____	_____
	Games/books	_____	_____
	Sunglasses	_____	_____
	Comb/Hairbrush	_____	_____
	Shampoo	_____	_____
	Sunscreen	_____	_____
	Insect repellent	_____	_____
	Wristwatch	_____	_____
	Tissues	_____	_____
Other			
	Medication	_____	_____
	Extra pair of prescription glasses	_____	_____

Appendix **5**

RESOURCES

American Camping Association
5000 State Road 67 North
Martinsville, IN 46151–7902
(765) 342–8456 (phone)
(765) 342–2065 (fax)
e-mail: aca@aca-camps.org
Web site: www.aca-camps.org

CAMP GUIDES

The Guide to ACA Acccredited Camps
(annual guide)
Available from ACA bookstore, (800) 428–CAMP

Peterson's Summer Opportunities for Kids and Teenagers
(annual guide)
Published by Peterson's Guides

SUGGESTED READING LIST FOR CAMPERS

Young Campers/Picture Books/Easy Readers

Arthur Goes to Camp
by Marc Brown
Little Brown & Company, 1984

The Berenstain Bears Go to Camp
by Stan and Jan Berenstain
Random House, 1982

Camp Big Paw
by Dough Cushman
Harper Trophy, 1993

Camp Rotten Time
by Mike Thaler
Troll, 1994

The Cut-Ups at Camp Custer
by James Marshall
Puffin, 1991

Danny and the Dinosaur Go to Camp
by Syd Hoff
Harpercrest, 1996

A Day at Damp Camp
by George Ella Lyon
Orchard Books, 1996

I Don't Want to Go to Camp
Eve Bunting
Boyds Mills Press, 1996

Pinky and Rex Go to Camp
James Howe
Atheneum, 1992

OLDER CAMPERS/CHAPTER BOOKS

Avoiding Homesickness: Sure-Fire Ways to Beat the Sleep-Away Camp Blues
by Bibi Schweitzer
Available for $5 from Visibility Enterprises,
6 Oak Avenue
Larchmont, NY 10538

The Berenstain Bears at Camp Crush (chapter book)
by Stan and Jan Berenstain
Random House, 1994

Camp Knock Knock
by Betsy Duffey
Yearling Book, 1996

The Camp Knock Knock Mystery
by Betsy Duffey
Yearling Book, 1997

Camp Sink or Swim
Gibbs Davis
Random House, 1997

The Great Summer Camp Catastrophe
by Jean Van Leeuwen
Dial Books, 1992

Upchuck Summer
by Joel L. Schwartz
Yearling Books, 1983

Upchuck Summer's Revenge
by Joel L. Schwartz
Yearling Books, 1990

Index